GEEK PROOF YOUR FAITH

HOW TO HANDLE 12 TOUGH ISSUES WITHOUT LOOKING STUPID

GREG JOHNSON & MICHAEL ROSS

ZondervanPublishingHouse

Grand Rapids, Michigan

A Division of HarperCollinsPublishers

Geek-Proof Your Faith: How to Handle 12 Tough Issues without Looking Stupid
Copyright © 1995 by Greg Johnson and Michael Ross

Requests for information should be addressed to:
Zondervan Publishing House
Grand Rapids, Michigan 49530

Library of Congress Cataloging-in-Publication Data

Johnson, Greg, 1956–
    Geek-proof your faith : how to handle 12 tough issues without looking
stupid / Greg Johnson and Michael Ross.
        p.   cm.
    Summary: Presents Christian perspectives on issues such as
evolution/creation, abortion, and the reliability of the Bible, and suggests
responses which teenagers may offer in communicating their faith.
    ISBN: 0-310-49541-5
    1. Apologetics—Juvenile literature. 2. Teenagers—Religious life. 3.
Christian life—Juvenile literature. [1. Christian life.] I. Ross, Michael,
1961–   . II. Title
BT1102.J64   1995
239—dc20   95-8266
                                                                       CIP
                                                                        AC

Edited by Robin Schmitt
Interior design by Sue Koppenol
Interior illustrations by Corbin Hillam

Printed in the United States of America

96 97 98 99 00 / ❖ DH/ 10 9 8 7 6 5 4 3 2

STUFF IN THIS BOOK

ASPIRING TO GEEKHOOD ... WITHOUT REALLY TRYING

It's easy being a geek. There are millions of them who don't even know they are one.

What IS a geek, you ask?

That depends, of course, on WHO you ask. Most would say, "A geek is someone who has taped their glasses together, wears dorky clothes, gets good grades, can't play sports, and basically is a social outcast with no hope of ever breaking into the cool group." Using that definition, it could well be said that some Christians ARE geeks.

But since you're sorta carrying on a conversation with us two guys, we've got a different definition. We believe "geeks" are actually real people. They have flesh and bones, a mind, feelings, the ability to love others and be hurt by others, a mom, dad, brother, sister, grandparents who think they're great ... and a future beyond high school. Oh yes, God also thought enough of them to send his Son to die for them.

That definition kinda puts a whole new face on those you may think are geeks. So let's define a geek this way: a real person who's often misunderstood.

There might not be anything more frustrating than being misunderstood, anything more demoralizing than people in your universe, people who matter to you, not knowing—or not wanting to know—the real you.

Ever felt that way as a Christian? Ever felt that you couldn't let others know the real you—especially the spiritual side of you? Have you ever been frustrated because you were too afraid to reveal to others the person inside, who really does believe what the Bible says, who's convinced that the human race is more than a cosmic accident?

If you have, then you're a Christian geek: a real, believing person who's often misunderstood.

It doesn't feel so hot, does it? Christians have struggled at times with having family and friends thinking weird thoughts about us. Our beliefs have been laughed at, our motives sometimes mistrusted . . . and we've felt the agony of defeat when it comes to communicating the most important thing—THE MOST IMPORTANT PERSON—in our lives. It is frustrating and demoralizing. Sometimes it's depressing.

What's the answer? To let people know we're real, and to get them to understand us, of course!

That's the goal of this book: to help you let others know and understand that you're a real person with real beliefs about a God who is crazy about you—and them. When you start reading these pages, you'll see that we're hitting two main areas where Christians are viewed as geeks:

IN THE CLASSROOM

We want you to know what to say—as well as how to say it—when your faith is challenged by teachers or classmates. There ARE answers to tough questions about what we believe. About half of this book will give you the tools you need to help you be understood. We've identified the situations where Christian students are commonly challenged (and sometimes ridiculed) for their faith. We've painted a ton of real-life scenarios about public school life, and hopefully given you a good start when it comes to verbally defending—or simply explaining—the real you.

It should be mentioned that there's a difference between being understood and being believed. Helping others *understand* where you're coming from is your responsibility. Getting someone to *believe* is up to God. It's his job to bring others into a relationship with him; it's our job to represent him as best we can.

IN YOUR LIFE

As a Christian, however, being understood is only half the battle. You see, many outside the church will not be too impressed with our great logic and well-thought-through answers to the tough issues of faith. To quote an old phrase: they want to see a sermon rather than hear one. And the way in which you live your life will speak louder than any perfectly delivered speech.

The fact is, some Christians are misunderstood because their lives don't come close to matching what they say they believe about God and the Bible. They are WORSE THAN geeks, because they're not acting like the REAL them: they're not showing what they really deep-down believe to be true. They treat themselves or others poorly, they're judgmental, and some honestly don't have a clue about what their lives are actually communicating.

This job—of living what we believe—is a lifetime assignment, and we need to realize we won't be perfect all the time. But we do need to take the next step up toward becoming more like Jesus Christ. That's all God wants, and that's all we're asking: take one more step up. Don't try to be "Super Saint," just try to improve, okay?

We're all geeks in some areas, but that doesn't mean we have to stay that way. As a Christian, use this book to start becoming less of a geek and more of a real, believing person who IS understood.

1

Flattening the Evolution Myth Without Getting Squashed

DID HUMANS EVOLVE FROM THE FLEA?

I (Mike) was heading through the supermarket checkout stand a while back, when POW! ... a headline from one of those zany tabloids jumped right off the page at me: "Stunning New Scientific Evidence Proves ... MAN DESCENDED FROM THE FLEA!"

"Say what?" I gasped. "Evidence? Proof? Who ACTUALLY believes this stuff?!"

Then a chilling thought shot through my mind. Every day in classrooms across the country, students just like you are having their own "close encounters of the equally weird kind."

Check out this scenario: Professor Petridish—your first-period science teacher—points to a big chart showing a hairy, apelike creature evolving into a hairless bodybuilder.

"My friends," he announces as he peels a banana and takes a bite, "these are your ancestors. You evolved from the ape. And the way you guys monkey around, I'm not surprised!"

While the room breaks up into laughter, your stomach knots up.

Why is he teaching this stuff as FACT? Why isn't creation-ism taken seriously? Should I speak up—or clam up?

ULTIMATE GEEK RESPONSES

- "Gimme a break, Mr. Know-it-all! Science hasn't proven a thing. In fact, most scientists are so blinded by their own egos and high IQs, they'd like us to think they're the ones responsible for the human race."
- "Wake up, class! Don't you see what's happening? Evolution is yet another trick of the Devil. It's an evil scheme designed to lead God's creation away from the Creator and down a path straight to . . . H-E-L-L!"
- "Okay, I admit it. Some of the stuff in the Bible sounds like major storybook material. I mean, really . . . the entire earth, and everything in it, glued together in just six days! I have my doubts. But I have my doubts about what you're teaching, too. So here's the deal. You believe whatever *you* think is right, and I'll do the same. Hey, don't step on my toes with *your* opinions."
- "EVOLUTION?! No way, dude. The only one in my family who even remotely

resembles a monkey is my sister. But trust me . . . with her moods, she's not of *this* world!"

A BETTER RESPONSE

We're convinced that the biblical perspective on human origins should be presented in the classroom—but not only by the teacher. By whom, then? By you, of course. Every Christian teen has a right to respectfully and responsibly share what he or she believes.

Following are some valuable tips—and a pretty good strategy—to help you stand firm . . . even when the pressure makes you squirm. Try this eight-key plan:

EIGHT KEYS TO UNLOCKING THE TRUTH
KEY #1: Don't argue, and don't try to act like "Mr. Expert"

Your goal should *never* be to blow a classmate or the teacher out of the water, show them up, or *prove* how wacko their arguments are. Your job is to share—in a logical manner—what you've learned from the Bible and from science, and to allow others to either accept it or reject it.

Since you probably *won't* change the teacher's mind, a good goal is to simply plant a seed of doubt so your classmates won't swallow the evolution theory without at least questioning it.

KEY #2: Get the facts straight
Evolutionists believe . . .

All life gradually evolved from a single cell, which evolved from dead matter (or perhaps some kind of "big bang"). In the beginning, there was only empty space. Then dust appeared on the scene, followed by gases and chemicals. Where did *they* come from? That's one mystery they haven't yet figured out. Eventually everything developed by millions of random changes over eons of time.

Many (but not all) scientists believe in the big bang theory, which supposedly took place about twenty billion years ago. They say that this material, as a result of gravity, gathered into a huge primordial cloud. After ages, it compressed into an immense, unbelievably hot ball, which finally exploded. This explosion flung these same elements into space. More eons later, gravity caused them to form into millions of smaller balls. And ages after that, they became stars, planets, galaxies. At some point, these heavenly bodies began rotating in space, in an incredibly accurate and predictable manner. All by random chance! This is a pretty fantastic theory, isn't it? But here's the strange deal: most people accept it as truth, without examining it. Why? Because that's what they've been taught from kindergarten up. But the truth is, it's only a theory—NOT scientific fact.

> "Fossils are a great embarrassment to evolutionary theory and offer strong support for the concept of Creation."
> GARY PARKER, PH.D.,
> BIOLOGIST-PALEONTOLOGIST
> AND FORMER EVOLUTIONIST

Creationists believe . . .

All life and our existence came by the acts of a living, loving Creator. Since their original inception, cells have built themselves from carefully designed and coded information that has been passed from one life to the next.

When Creationists refer to the term "Creation," they are speaking of the original creation of the cosmos—a cosmos in fully working form. Many Creationists accept the Bible's historical account, which describes a unique, one-time creation event that took one week and resulted in a complete world, including sea and land, trees, moon, stars, fish, birds, land animals, and man (all fully formed, in that order). Some Christians would say that all this happened in one week; others would say that a "day"—as written in the Bible—could be thousands of years (2 Peter 3:8).

Understand that all Christians do not agree on God's method of creation. Did he create the universe in one week, or did he use an evolutionary process to accomplish his goal?

It is beyond the scope of this chapter to attempt to account for *every* theory that Bible-believing Christians hold. Our purpose is to give you ideas that will help you—and others—question the "facts" taught in most public schools. (For further research, please see the suggested reading that is listed in the back of this book.)

KEY #3: Look closely at what evolutionists are arguing

Despite all the scientific gobbledygook, there are two basic definitions you should know: *microevolution* and *macroevolution*. (It's not really that complicated, so hang with us!)

Scientists studying microevolution can observe small changes within different types of living organisms. This perspective is valid and actually in line with biblical teaching. In fact, it's not really evolution at all. Dogs will interbreed, and the world will end up with a new breed of dog. But this dog is still a dog.

So what evolutionists refer to as microevolution—change within a created kind—was orchestrated by God to help preserve life. In some ways it's a survival characteristic. Different species experience *small changes* so that they can adapt to a *changing environment*. But they are not transforming into a different species.

On the other hand, macroevolution suggests that—over millions of years—a dog could evolve into, say, a horse. And that an ape (or a flea, if you believe the tabloids) could one day become a person.

Evolutionists who hold this view claim that the original clump in the primordial soup became a cell, somehow got life, then divided. One cell ended up on land and became the ancient ancestor of plant life. The other cell stayed in the water to eventually evolve into boneless sea creatures. After millions of years, one of these creatures—by random chance—became a fish with a backbone. And that, these evolutionists say, is the real beginning of humankind.

Something isn't adding up. Of course, advocates of this viewpoint wouldn't agree. They point to what they claim is their proof: fossil records. Fossils are ancient forms of plant and animal life embedded in sedimentary rock in the crust of the earth, and they are found all over the world. There are "graveyards" that contain the fossilized bones of dinosaurs and other huge animals and birds, as well as those of smaller animals (including apes and early man).

In 1974 scientists claimed they discovered the long-sought "missing link" between apes and humans. An expedition to Ethiopia led by Donald Johanson, president of the Institute of Human Origins, painstakingly pieced together a remarkable ancient primate skeleton. Although about sixty percent of the skeleton—including much of the skull—was missing, the scientists believed that the apelike primate had some characteristics that were significantly humanlike. They named this "proof" Lucy (or in scientific jargon, *Australopithecus afarensis*).

KEY #4: Ask for proof of macroevolutionism

Know what you'll get? You guessed it: Z-I-P. The truth is, macroevolutionism is a theory with *no evidence*.

Check out the observations of Charles Darwin—one of the world's early advocates of evolutionism, and a staunch defender of the "macro" view. In Darwin's own words: "As by this theory innumerable transitional forms must have existed, why do we not find them embedded in countless numbers in the crust of the earth?"

In other words, for macroevolution to be true, scientists would have to unearth fossils showing a gradual, step-by-step development of lower animal life into more and more complex forms. No such fossils exist. The millions found

> "Nature never taught me that there exists a God of glory and infinite majesty. I had to learn that in other ways. But nature gave the word 'glory' a meaning for me. I still do not know where else I could have found one."
> C. S. LEWIS

are all of highly complex forms of life. The absence of fossil records (of transitional species) proves that it hasn't happened, current observation proves that it is not happening today, and genetic research proves that it could never happen. In other words, a dog just can't evolve into a horse, and an ape can't develop into a man.

Hmmm ... even "Mr. Macroevolution" himself couldn't find evidence to support his claims!

KEY #5: Point out that macroevolutionism is not scientific fact

Crack open any basic biology textbook and pinpoint the traditional definition of the *scientific method*: "Principles and procedures for the systematic pursuit of knowledge, involving the recognition and formulation of a problem, the collection of data through observation and experimentation, and the formulation and testing of hypotheses." (Translation: if you can't duplicate it in a laboratory, you can't call it scientific.)

Next locate the definition of a *scientific hypothesis*: "An unproved assumption."

Now point to the fact that since macroevolution cannot be observed or measured (partly because of the lack of a fossil record), it's just a theory, and can only be presented as speculation—*not fact.*

KEY #6: Show the logic of creationism

The evidence needed to support creationism is a fossil record that shows complex life appearing suddenly— with no fossils that show lower animals developing into new and complex forms of life.

Guess what? That's exactly what scientists have discovered. They've learned that throughout history, higher categories of living things—fishes, reptiles, primates (including man)—appeared on the scene abruptly.

God's Awesome Creation

Think deeply about the origins of life and ask yourself this question: how could this mind-boggling universe, with all of its intricacies, come into being just by chance? Take man, for example. The human body is a marvelously constructed and complex machine. Examine the most visible part of the body: the skin. In magnified pictures, you can see skin layers, blood vessels, oil glands, hair roots, pores, nerves, and pigment.

> "When I make an incision with my scalpel, I see organs of such intricacy that there simply hasn't been enough time for natural evolutionary processes to have developed them."
>
> C. EVERETT KOOP,
> FORMER U.S. SURGEON GENERAL

One fourth of all the bones in the body are in the hand. With the hand, an artist can do the most delicate painting, and a construction worker can lift heavy beams. Each fingerprint is individual.

Study the digestive system and see how everything works together: the pancreas, liver, gallbladder, lymph glands. And think about how the eyes work. Or what about the brain? It's so complicated that even the most complex computer comes nowhere near its efficiency. Not only does the brain control the body, but we use it to think and create, to put people in outer space, to feel, to love, and (with the brain and the spirit) to reach out to God.

So the question is, how could such complex and coordinating systems happen by random chance . . . then evolve over millions of years?

KEY #7: Point out the second law of thermodynamics

This scientific law of physics states that all things run down, not up. Anything left unattended falls apart.

How does this relate to the evolutionism-creationism debate? Since living and nonliving things gradually break down and become more disorganized as time passes, it's illogical to believe that matter could have had the capacity to go from a nonliving, disorganized state to a living, organized one.

The fact is, all uphill processes (such as growth) are temporary and require a separate, intelligent force to put it into motion. (Get the picture?)

KEY #8: Lastly, drive home your point with a handy word picture—the "airplane comparison"

Question: What part of an airplane flies? Is it the fuselage? The cockpit? The wings? The wheels?

Answer: No *single* part can fly. In reality, an airplane is a collection of nonflying parts. The only thing that flies is the total, organized airplane.

Key point: These nonflying parts have no capacity to organize themselves into an airplane—*somebody had to do it.*

Now, connect your word picture with a living cell.

Question: What part of a cell is alive? The protoplasm? The cell wall? The nucleus?

Answer: No *single* part of a cell is alive. A living cell is a collection of nonliving parts. The only thing that makes the cell alive is the total organization of nonliving parts.

Key point: These nonliving parts have no capacity to organize themselves into a living cell. Therefore it's logical to say *somebody had to do it.* (That somebody, of course, is God.)

Conclusion: The whole issue of the origin of man is primarily a faith issue and can't be proven with observable, scientific facts. But the truth is, creationism is more in tune with the laws of science than evolutionism is.

This kind of reasoning casts severe doubt on the idea that life could have formed itself. The Christian faith is not a blind faith. It's a reasonable faith that's based on logic. And this point of view should be represented in a classroom.

TERMS TO KNOW

Big Bang According to one cosmological theory, the violent cosmic explosion at an infinitesimally small point from which the universe originated billions of years ago.

Entropy A measure of the disorder in a system. Since the law of entropy states that a closed system evolves toward a state of maximum entropy, critics of evolutionary theory point out that the increasing order and complexity involved in evolution would require some kind of outside, intelligent influence.

Evolutionary Naturalism The belief that the world can be understood only through the application of evolutionary science and that no account needs to be taken of supernatural or spiritual forces.

Fossil Record A record of the fossilized remains of various organisms, arranged in a "geological column" in a manner that—conventional science asserts—broadly reflects the evolution of species. Creationist critics of conventional science claim that the fossil record is inconsistent and not complete enough to warrant this conclusion.

Hypothesis A provisional explanation for a natural phenomenon. For a hypothesis to have scientific value, it must account for most of the relevant data, and—at least in theory—it must be subject to disproof.

Macroevolution Evolutionary change that involves large and complex steps (such as the transformation of one species into another).

Microevolution Limited genetic changes at the species or subspecies level.

Natural Selection According to evolutionary theory, the process by which organisms with traits that better enable them to adapt to environmental factors (such as predators or scarcity of food) will survive and reproduce in greater numbers.

ON YOUR OWN

1. Read Genesis 1:1–2:25. Why, do you think, do non-Christian scientists reject this account of creation?

2. Jot down things about the story of creation that are hard to accept. Where does faith fit in?

3. Think about how incredible your body is. Next think about the world, then the universe. Now focus on the Creator. Read Isaiah 40:26 and spend a few minutes jotting down all the mind-boggling things that God created.

4. Read Isaiah 45:18, Romans 1:25, and Ephesians 2:10, then complete the following:
   - ✎ What do these verses say about God?
   - ✎ What do they communicate about the human race?
   - ✎ Name one reason why God created people.

5. Read Psalm 148. Make a list of the things you are thankful that God created.

WITH A GROUP

1. Has the theory of evolution poked holes in the biblical account of creation? Why or why not?
2. Why does it take just as much faith to buy the evolution theory as it does to believe in creationism? Is evolutionism actually just a religion?
3. Have you given much thought to dinosaurs and how they fit into the picture?
4. If you were asked to give proof of creationism, how would you respond?
5. Give three reasons you believe why creationism should and should not be taught in public schools.

   Should:
   - ✎
   - ✎
   - ✎

   Should Not:
   - ✎
   - ✎
   - ✎

2

Secrets of a Funnatic Friendship

Jason yanks the hamburger out of Brock's hand and takes a bite. "Go on, banana brain . . . ask her," he mumbles, then opens his mouth and exposes the contents.

"GROSS! You just nuked my lunch, gorilla breath."

Eric slams his algebra book on Brock's fries—WHAM!—and scrapes the remains into a nearby trash can. "*That's* what I call gross," he grins.

"You're history," Brock snaps. "I'm gonna rip your lungs out through your armpits and knock your—"

The guys freeze as a herd of freshman goddesses rumble by.

"MAJOR babe city," Eric blurts.

Jason falls on his knees and goes into his Porky Pig routine. "P-p-p-please, Brocksters, you just g-g-g-gotta help us!"

"Not even," Brock snaps. "With you rejects around, I'm not goin' anywhere near those girls!"

"But they talk to you."

"And with your help, they might even talk to us," Eric adds.

"I'd rather eat maggot intestines."

"You're my best friend," Jason pleads.

"Friends help each other," Eric interjects.

"They don't kill a guy's lunch."

Jason holds up a french fry. "My last one. Take it."

Brock's eyes light up. A grin slowly forms on his lips. He flicks a french fry off Eric's book, then high-fives Jason. "Deal!"

LISA AND THE GOSSIP GANG

Lisa's face flushed as Heather filled her in on the latest gossip from Shelly.

"I hate her," Lisa exploded. "I can't believe she's spreading those lies. I hate Shelly so much I could strangle her, and I think I would if I had the chance."

"And I thought you two were best friends," Marsha said.

"Yeah, girl," Heather interjected. "Aren't you, like, twins . . . we don't see one without the other?"

Lisa practically choked on her burger. "Us . . . best friends! Get real. I'd rip her eyes out right now if she came around here."

RINNNGG.

The lunch bell sent the girls off to home economics. Lisa swung by her locker to snag her textbook. She fished out a couple of pens and slammed the door shut. *How* dare *that Shelly,* Lisa thought. *She may be popular with the quarterbacks; she may be Miss Cheerleader . . . but just who does she think she is?*

Lisa trotted down the hall, shot around the corner, then stopped.

"Hey there, Lisa," Shelly squeaked, throwing her arms around Lisa.

"Oh, uh . . . hi, Shelly." Lisa flashed a grin, then brushed her hair out of her eyes. "So, uh, how's my . . . friend doin' today?"

"Couldn't be better." Shelly pressed in closer to Lisa. "Hey, have I got some juicy news about Heather. Come by my house after school, okay? Let's invite a few of the girls over . . . We'll have a great time!"

"Ah, sure . . . after school . . . a few *friends* . . . Wouldn't miss it!"

This is *friendship*?

Hanging out with the Three Stooges at a toxic waste dump would be less hazardous. Sometimes friends treat each other more like Curly, Larry, and Moe than like . . . *friends*.

Leave it to your pals to do dumb things at the worst possible moments.

Guys: Your friends belch right when the best-looking girl at school finally says hi, pull pranks that aren't funny, and spill pop all over your new basketball shoes—then blame it on someone else.

Girls: Your friends blab secrets when they shouldn't, make you feel like crawling into the nearest hole when your boyfriend comes around, and sometimes make you wonder if being a hermit isn't such a bad option.

But face it everybody . . . you wouldn't have it any other way, right? You take a few jabs and risk some bruises now and then because friendship's important.

When push comes to shove, most friends stick with you better than the gooiest slice of pepperoni pizza. Your buddies also help you blast the boredom bug—they're good for more laughs (and screams) than the world's fastest, triple-looping roller coaster. And whether or not you realize it, they help you grow and learn more about yourself. Sometimes the only way to figure out what you're really thinking or feeling is to talk things out with a friend. And when you're with your friends, you can be yourself; it doesn't matter if you drool or have a big wad of gum stuck in your ear.

But friendships aren't always smooth sailing. The constant "playful" jabs sometimes start to sting . . . and somebody gets hurt. And like Lisa, there are too many times when our lips flap before our brains kick in.

Here's what's even worse: at times, it's hard to pick out the Christian kid from the crowd. Some churchgoing teens hide their faith—playing "secret agent" on campus—and often don't behave any differently than their non-Christian peers.

What kind of friend are you? And when the pressure's on, how do you react?

MARSHELLA'S MEGASIZED MESS

During lunch, Marshella didn't feel like eating with her friends on the lawn—the cool spot to hang out. She slipped into the school cafeteria and tried to blend in with the crowd.

As she unwrapped her cheeseburger, she noticed Megan at a nearby table. *She looks pitiful,* Marshella thought.

Megan sat alone, with her nose stuck into a large textbook. Without batting an eye, she mechanically reached into a sack with her right hand and pulled out food. Marshella noticed how that same hand trembled whenever someone nearby verbally hit her with an insult.

Oh Lord, I guess she's not that bad, Marshella began to pray. *If she would just comb her hair. And those clothes! Why does she wear those Brady Bunch outfits? She's definitely the kinda person Pastor Jeff is always preaching about in youth group: "Learn to be an ultimate 'Jesus-style' friend to EVERY-ONE."* Marshella got up and made her way toward Megan's table. *Here I go, God. This is my chance to—*

"Hi Marshella! Whatcha doin' in here?" her friend Deanna interrupted.

Marshella's body jerked. "Oh, hi . . . ahhh, just eating another gourmet lunch."

Deanna flashed a mocking grin. "Looked like you were about to talk to Megan. I don't understand you. Do you actually like her?!"

"Like her? Well . . . ahhh . . ." Suddenly Marshella couldn't think straight.

Deanna folded her arms. "Frankly, I'm getting the feeling that your taste in friends has gone to the . . . GEEKS!"

"NO, Deanna. I DON'T like her, okay?"

"Then help us pull a friendly little prank on Ms. Mega Mess?"

"Prank? What are you up to, Deanna?"

"Derek wants you to invite her to a skating party this weekend. We'll put her on wheels and watch her thrash around the rink. It should be good for a lot of laughs!"

"I don't know, Deanna—"

"Thought you weren't a megageek fan!"

Marshella's heart raced. Deanna's friendship was important to her, but she knew it was wrong to hurt others. *If I do it, I could never live with myself. But if I don't, it's social suicide for sure. Lord, HELP!*

ULTIMATE GEEK RESPONSES

- "Hey, I'm in. Think I'm a megageek fan!?" Then justify to yourself later: *Look, I can't commit social suicide. And anyway, this girl doesn't have friends . . . so it doesn't matter. After all, I'm the one who has the most to lose. My rep is on the line.*
- Agree to pull the prank, then apologize to Megan later.
- "Ahh . . . I can't. I just remembered an important family outing that day. My aunt is sick and we have to visit her. Yeah, that's it. But otherwise I'd love to join in on the fun."

A BETTER RESPONSE

Understand the facts of friendship:

A true friend is	A true friend is NOT
someone who accepts you just the way you are (despite a few jabs)	someone who constantly aims his or her word-bullets at you
someone you trust	someone who jams when the going gets rough
someone who sticks up for you	someone who's phony
someone who listens	someone who uses you
someone who really cares	someone who lies
someone who tries to model Jesus	someone who doesn't care about modeling Jesus

FRIENDSHIP FACT: PALS HANG OUT IN HERDS

Name a torture that's worse than eating creamed spinach, and more humiliating than one of Aunt Edna's big, wet Christmas kisses. Answer: sitting in a crowded cafeteria . . . ALONE!

Hands down, this is worse than a dozen wet kisses—maybe even worse than death itself. Enter a room filled with grinning faces you don't recognize (especially if you're the new kid on campus) and your stomach knots up. Your knees shake, your mouth feels like it's full of peanut butter, and that cool new T-shirt suddenly looks like it made a trip through a steam bath.

As you look around the room, you notice something strange (definitely Twilight Zone material): everybody is hanging out in herds, or cliques—small, exclusive clumps of guys and girls who share the same interests. Keep looking—you'll see all kinds of herds: jocks, surfers, skateboarders, science buffs, metalheads, drama dudes, even . . . GEEKS!

You already know friendship is important. But why does it feel so weird to do a solo step? And just why do guys and girls hang out in herds, anyway?

One word: acceptance. No one wants to be left out. When a small group of friends takes you in, you don't have to worry about being alone.

Are herds bad? Well . . . yes and no.

Jesus hung out with a herd: those who followed him. They often met by themselves for prayer, teaching, and good times. But whenever outsiders came along, the group opened up to them. Jesus was not selective in whom he befriended—he accepted everyone.

If your herd slams the door on strangers and alienates others (makes them feel like aliens), it's time to quit being a geek and head for better pasture. Hang out with guys and girls you feel comfortable with, but don't build huge walls around your group. Reach out.

FINDING THE RIGHT HERD

Just about the time the school year kicks into high gear (usually right around midterms), you've probably settled into a pack of pals that you'll stay with for the rest of the year. But how can you be sure you'll be able to keep them? How can you be a positive influence on your herd?

"The best way to *have* a good friend is to *be* a good friend." This is a very old proverb, but it's still true today.

If you want to stop clashing and start firming up some solid friendships, remember these important facts:

You're not alone. The people you hang out with have exactly the same pressures and problems as you. Let them know that you respect them and that they're important to you.

Get real! People will see right through you if you're phony. Be the kind of person others can trust, by being honest with yourself and with them.

Give a grin. Smiles are important: they enable you to communicate acceptance without saying a word. So guys, when your friend is having an especially bad day, pop a breath mint, pucker up, and smack him in the kisser with a super-slobbery, Aunt Edna-style smooch. (Just kidding, of course.) If that's not your style—or if he's bigger than you—a friendly slap on the back will do.

Learn to care. Too often, people put themselves before others. But learn to do just the opposite. Reach out to your buddies and put their needs first. Being sensitive to the feelings of others is a skill. Horsing around is one thing, but constantly hurling insults or laughing at people's mistakes can hurt. When a tough time hits, they'll remember who *not* to go to.

Though it seems like it's against the law for a teen to treat someone right, you'll be surprised at how many friends you can make—and keep—by being understanding. By covering for others when they mess up—and trying not to make them feel foolish—you may end up with a life-long friendship. The key involves:

Turning off your tongue. Be a good listener. Ask a question, then close your mouth and show them that you're interested.

Watching those wounding words. If words can be weapons, they also can bring a healing touch. Say something positive to your friend. Be different and make it a habit to toss out compliments instead of put-downs.

WHEN A FRIEND BREAKS FROM THE HERD

Sometimes friends will try anything to be accepted— even by another group.

Face it, guys and girls . . . you want to be popular. So a few of your peers—or maybe even you—might compromise once, then maybe a second or third time. Before they know it, they slip right over the edge—and right into trouble. Some convince themselves, "I gotta look cool. Besides, this may be my last chance to move up and be really happy."

Know a friend who's slipping? One of the hardest parts about being a friend is helping your friend when he's moved into a group heading for turbulent waters. It's tough, but it's one of the most loving things you can do.

Make sure you affirm your friend and reject the action. Tell him you care about him and that it hurts to see him doing what he's doing. You can say, "It's your choice. If you want to continue doing these crazy things, go ahead. But I think it's stupid!" Let him know you're willing to be his friend no matter what.

Here are some ways you can steer a pal in the right direction:

- Talk to your parents or youth leader. Get their advice first.
- Pray. Ask Jesus to show you what to do, and ask him to use you as his tool.
- Go to your friend alone and talk. See if he or she will get back together with the right group.
- Listen to what your friend has to say. If he or she asks for your opinion, be honest and give it.

- Even if your troubled friend calls you names or laughs at you, keep your friendship open. What your mixed-up pal needs most are *real* friends who really care.
- If necessary, ask God to help *you* forgive your friend.

REMEMBER: YOU ARE AN AMBASSADOR OF CHRIST

Therefore, if anyone is in Christ, he is a new creation; the old has gone, the new has come! All this is from God, who reconciled us to himself through Christ and gave us the ministry of reconciliation: that God was reconciling the world to himself in Christ, not counting men's sins against them. And he has committed to us the message of reconciliation. We are therefore Christ's ambassadors, as though God were making his appeal through us. We implore you on Christ's behalf: Be reconciled to God.

2 CORINTHIANS 5:17–20

What kind of example are you? Whether you realize it or not, your actions are being watched by everybody around you. People hear what you say, and they see what you do, where you go, how you dress, and how you handle victory and defeat. You are Christ's example to others.

Check out Brent's story. This Minnesota teen grew up thinking he was nothing but a zero:

"When I was in seventh grade, I detested myself because I was obese," Brent said. "I remember sitting at home one night and taking a wire clothes hanger and beating myself on the thigh until I had big welts. I hated myself.

"But then I met a very special Christian teacher who showed me that God loves me just the way I am. I desperately wanted to see Jesus in the life of somebody. I wanted someone to put their arms around me, and I wanted to know that those were Jesus's arms. I liked the way my teacher represented God. Through him, I met God."

Remember: you don't have to be a Billy Graham or a "Super Christian" to be a good ambassador. By your life, you can point others to the Truth, the Way, and the Life.

GEEK-PROOFING YOUR FRIENDSHIPS BEGINS WITH Y-O-U

So just where is Jesus in your friendships? Do you take him to school with you? Do others see a reflection of him in your life?

"I saw him through my teacher's kind words and affirming smile," Brent said. "And despite all the bad stuff I'd heard about myself, I slowly learned that I was okay. Because Jesus made me. Even 'fat,' 'slob' *me!*"

But life's pressures can be immense. On some days, you wake up and don't feel very Christian. That's when you need to get near the heart of God. And this brings us to another key to geek-proofing your friendships. It can be summed up in one word: growth.

Okay, okay . . . so you may have seen this cute little acronym in youth group. But hey, it works! So hang with us and check out this six-step G.R.O.W.T.H. plan to success:

TIP #1: **G**o . . . and keep your appointments with God

Do you have a regular quiet time with Jesus? In any relationship, communication is important. Make an effort to spend time alone with God every day. Go to him daily in prayer. Tell the Lord how much you love him, and talk about your friends and their needs. Develop a consistent prayer time, a time when you come to him with your praise, your adoration, and your thanksgiving. Also go to the Lord with your needs.

Be totally honest with God. He knows what you're thinking and what's going on. Tell God about your struggles, and he'll be there to help you.

TIP #2: Read

Get into God's Word daily. Study the Scriptures, memorize verses, and think about how to apply them. As you do this, a ton of great stuff gets imprinted on your heart. Try reading a verse or chapter each night before you go to bed. It'll give your mind something to work on while you sleep. Make this a daily habit.

TIP #3: Obey

Make every effort to obey what you've read and to follow God's commandments.

TIP #4: Witness

Let your life be an example to others. Seek to honor God in all you do. When the Lord gives you the opportunities, be ready to give a defense for the hope that is in you (1 Peter 3:15).

TIP #5: Trust ... that God will never leave you

Nor will he forsake you. He will always be there with you.

TIP #6: Hang out ... with friends who share your values

This is another way you can grow in God and avoid unnecessary pressure. If your friends are doing things you know are wrong, make sure they don't drag you down with them. You might even consider not hanging out with them.

ON YOUR OWN

1. Add to the following list of famous friends:

Snoopy	and	Woodstock
Tom Sawyer	and	Huck Finn
Batman	and	Robin
_____	and	_____

_____ and _____

_____ and _____

> ✎ What qualities make a friend an absolute, without-a-doubt, one-hundred-percent TRUE friend?

2. Read John 15:9–17. Name some qualities about Jesus that make him the ultimate best friend.

3. Read John 13:1–17. From this passage, how did Jesus influence others during the time when he walked on this earth?

> ✎ Name some ways that you, as a Christian, can have a positive influence on your friends.

4. Read Proverbs 27:10 and Ecclesiastes 4:10. Why is it important to have friends and be a friend?

5. Jot down the name of a friend who really needs you in his or her life:

Now make a covenant with God to be a prayer warrior in this person's life.

Lord, I am making a commitment to pray for _____ on a regular basis. I will also do my best to be a solid, Christian example in my friend's life by putting his or her needs first and by helping my friend grow in his or her walk with you.

_____   _____
Your Name   Date

WITH A GROUP

1. Name a person you'd "lay down your life for" (John 15:13). Why would you do this?

2. What's the single greatest way you can help a friend?

3. Have someone in the group read Matthew 5:43–48.

   ✎ Why is it hard to love those who don't love you back?

   ✎ Think of someone in your life who has been hard to love. Now share with the group some ways that you can be his or her friend.

4. Name a time when following the herd got you into trouble.

   ✎ Did you end up compromising your values?

   ✎ What messages about you did your actions send to others?

5. Name some actions or situations that destroy trust in a friendship.

   ✎ What are some prime trust-builders?

3

Bucking the Bible Blasters

"So, Mark. What's that book with the gold pages, the one on the bottom of our locker? Something for English?"

"Uh . . . no, Ramon. It's a Bible."

"A Bible? No way! I didn't think anyone read that book except grandmas and TV preachers. What's in it?"

"All kinds of stuff. History, poetry, stories about men and women who lived thousands of years ago."

"Sounds pretty boring. Who makes you bring it to school?"

"No one."

"Then why would you ever want to lug it here? Besides, shouldn't you keep it at home? After all, this is a public school, and there is such a thing as separation of church and state. . . . Not that I really care."

"Actually, there's nothing illegal about bringing a Bible to school, Ramon. Just because it's a public school doesn't mean I can't read what I want to in my spare time. Have you ever read any of it?"

"Me? No way. You kiddin'? I'm not religious. Looks like you are, though."

"I'm not really religious. I'm a Christian. There's a big difference. Want to hear about it sometime?"

"Sorry, Mark, I'm not into it. Here comes Kathy. Ask her, maybe she is. Hey, Kathy. Ol' Mark here has a Bible, and he's trying to tell me he's not religious. You ever hear of that?"

UUGGHH! Not Kathy. Now she'll never talk to me. Lord, is this the price of bringing my Bible to school? What if word gets around? Everyone's going to think I'm "religious."

ULTIMATE GEEK RESPONSES

- "Um . . . hi, Kathy. Ramon was just being an A-number-one jerk here, trying to tell me I couldn't bring my Bible to school. Have you ever known someone so ignorant?"
- "I gotta get to class."
- "Listen, Ramon. The Bible is GOD's WORD. You know what that means, bucko? It means that ignorant sots like you are going to fuel the fires of hell unless you start reading it. And even though you're gorgeous, Kathy, the Bible doesn't say that your good looks are going to get you to heaven. You both better listen to me while there's still time, or you'll be pickin' hot embers out of your hair for a few million years."
- "Hi, Kathy. Ramon's giving me a hard time for bringing my Bible *one time* to school. That doesn't make me religious. Besides, I brought it to show

my English teacher *(lying).* Hey, you going to the
game this Friday?"

SOCIAL SUICIDE?

Unfortunately, the last thing most teens want is to be
a dead giveaway. Especially when it comes to the religious
label, which sometimes blackballs Christians from a social
life with the cool crowd. After all, what would you think
about some Moslem who brought the Koran to school and
started carrying it around? You'd probably think he or she
was a religious weirdo, right?

Most people who have no Christian background think
the Bible is a boring old book with too many words and not
enough pictures. On the surface, they're right. It doesn't
exactly resemble *Nintendo Power, YM,* or *Sports Illustrated.*

Defending the Bible against skeptics may be the
toughest dilemma—yet the most important issue—a
Christian high schooler has to "geek-proof." Friends will
give you weird looks or ask tough questions you really don't
know how to answer. Some of their questions will even be
pretty good ones (that is, you may not have the answer
right at your fingertips):

- Wasn't the Bible written too long ago to really
  be relevant today?
- Why do so many parts seem to not make any
  sense?
- Are you sure it's historically accurate?
- Aren't there some errors in the Bible?

While we can give sound reasons for believing that the
Bible is actually God's Word (which is one goal of this
chapter), don't expect your average pre-Christian to buy
into this conviction. Here's why:

1. Movies and television don't exactly put the Bible
   or Christians on a high pedestal. Most of the

time, Christians are the brunt of jokes or made to look like crazed Iranian religious fanatics.

2. If your classmates are not Christians, you can likely conclude that their parents aren't, either. That may mean these students have already heard a bunch of negative stuff about the church and about pastors, priests, and Christians in general.

3. Perhaps your friends have had a bad experience with "religion." Since Christians are human—and do make mistakes—there's a good chance your friends have seen or heard something that turned them off.

There's not much you can do if these three things are clouding their ability to look at the Bible without biases, but you can be ready to talk about why you hold the Bible in high regard, if they ask.

REASONS GOD GAVE US THE BIBLE

A guy once told me (Greg) to try to convince him about Christianity without using the Bible. He truly believed there was nothing of value in it. The reason? It couldn't answer *every one* of his questions about *every* subject.

What were God's intentions when he gave us his Word?

To show us his true character. By choosing to send his only Son to die on a cross for our sins, he exemplified true, unselfish love. The central theme of the entire Bible—Old Testament and New Testament—is this: God used the Jewish people to bring forth the Messiah, who would save *all* people.

To give us an "owner's manual" for getting the most out of life. To place us on Earth and allow us to make it up as we go would have been cruel beyond belief. God's guidelines for how we are to treat each other and how we can get to know him better are perfectly clear. The Bible is one hundred percent accurate in everything God felt was important for us to know. While there is room for debate on irrelevant issues (like whether Judas hanged himself or whether he stabbed himself—see "Resolving 'Contradictions' in the Bible" at the end of the book), there are no discrepancies in his promises, commands, and warnings—the most important stuff we need to know.

THINGS THE BIBLE WASN'T DESIGNED TO ANSWER

Science. Should the Bible be the final word on subjects like these: What really happened to dinosaurs? How do you cause nuclear fission? How many solar systems are there? Why does the sun set in the west? How do you cure heart disease?

While these are important questions to some, God decided they didn't contribute to his overall plan to reveal himself to humans, so he left them out. Like a father giving his final message to his wife and kids before he goes off to war, God gave us the things we needed to know *the most* through the Bible.

History. Do we need a year-by-year, detailed, one hundred percent infallible description of history in order to believe he created us for a reason? Again, that would be great for us to have, but it wouldn't change the central theme.

How accurate is Bible history? If you skim through the Old Testament, you can see that it mentions many matters of a historical nature: kings, rulers, peoples, nations, confederacies, military campaigns, political customs, and great battles. It would be ridiculous to assume that every solitary historical reference in the Bible has had confirmation from an outside, impartial source. But archaeologists and researchers are constantly making new discoveries that confirm Bible history.

Geography. If God wanted to prove his existence, why didn't he make the Bible say things like "The world is round . . . The Garden of Eden can be found in . . . Noah's ark is really on Mount . . . The world's tallest mountain is Mount Everest"?

Do you need to know this stuff to realize that God loves you enough to send his only Son to die on a cross and pay the penalty for your sin? We hope not.

Whenever people have had access to good data on science, history, and geography from other sources that were in turn authoritative, we have never been able to find any Scriptural discrepancies that stand the test of time. When the Bible does speak on these subjects, it is authoritative. Actually, trying to cross-reference what we know compared to what God knows is like authenticating time from the Greenwich Observatory (where the world's official time is kept) by checking it against a $2.69 digital watch bought at a gas station. He knows infinitely more than us. In truth, it's arrogant for humans to believe that God should have to prove himself to us by being a detailed historian.

THE BIBLE IS UNIQUE

- It features sixty-six books by forty authors (from every walk of life, including kings, peasants, philosophers, fishermen, poets, statesmen, scholars), yet it is totally consistent.
- It has had a tremendous influence on people.
- It was written over a period of sixteen hundred years, on three continents (Asia, Africa, Europe).
- Parts of it have been preserved for over four thousand years.
- It answers people's deepest questions—about purpose, death, eternity.
- It is archaeologically accurate.

- In the Old Testament, there are 318 prophecies about the Messiah that were all fulfilled by Jesus.
- The modern translations of the New Testament are extremely accurate and reliable. By way of comparison, in every one of Shakespeare's thirty-seven plays (in existence just over two hundred years), there are approximately one hundred readings still in dispute, many of which materially

How Was the New Testament Put Together?

Back in the 1800s, ancient Greek texts of the New Testament were divided by scholars into "families." The scholars had noticed that some manuscripts had similar characteristics, based on what part of the world they were discovered in.

The major families are: Alexandrian (Egypt), Byzantine (Turkey), Caesarean (Israel), and Western (Roman). The families given the most weight in terms of authority are those which are shorter, more difficult, and more ancient (mainly the Alexandrian texts). The Byzantine texts are in more abundance, but they are longer readings (meaning that scribes added words as they copied), and they are not as old.

But even between these four families, there is no discrepancy in the meaning of the texts. Any discrepancy that does exist is just a matter of a few peripheral words.

affect the meaning of the passages in which they occur.

HOW CAN YOU BE SURE THE NEW TESTAMENT REALLY IS ACCURATE AND RELIABLE?

There are more than 5,330 Greek New Testament parchment fragments still in existence, some dating within a century of the apostles. Also, we have some eight thousand Latin parchments, and hundreds more in dozens of other ancient versions. (It should be noted that there are still this many intact despite the fact that the Roman emperor Diocletian had a standing order that all Scriptures be burned if discovered. Many Christians chose to die rather than "deny the faith" by surrendering New Testament Scriptures for destruction.)

As further corroboration to New Testament accuracy, within two hundred years, all but eleven verses of the New Testament were quoted by early church fathers, in 36,289 citations.

Are all of the passages in these scraps of parchment the same, word for word? Actually, no. But that isn't a cause for alarm. If *you* copied a book of the Bible, then checked it with your original, you'd find a few misspellings, and *a*'s turned into *the*'s. Does this mean that the text's message is different or that you messed up an essential doctrine of the faith? Not likely.

Scholars *are* certain of the *exact* wording of all but four hundred words in the New Testament. Nearly all of these are tense issues, minor word changes, and a few added words that assist in clarity for that particular language.

Let's look at the writings of some men in early history— men about whose existence historians have absolutely no doubt —and compare them to the New Testament:

Person	Lived (Wrote)	Earliest Copy	Number of Copies of Writings in Existence
Caesar (*The Gallic Wars)*	100–44 B.C.	A.D. 900	10
Homer (*The Odyssey, The Iliad)*	900 B.C.	A.D. 1400	643
Sophocles (Greek dramatist)	496–406 B.C.	A.D. 950	193
Euripides (Greek dramatic poet)	480–406 B.C.	A.D. 1180	9
Plato (Greek philosopher)	427–347 B.C.	A.D. 940	7
Aristotle (Greek philosopher)	384–322 B.C.	A.D. 1100	5
Demosthenes (orator)	384–322 B.C.	A.D. 860	200
Lucretius (Roman poet and philosopher)	96–55 B.C.	A.D. 930	2
Livy (Roman historian)	59 B.C.–A.D. 17	A.D. 500	20
New Testament	A.D. 40–100	A.D. 130	14,000

Check the encyclopedia in your school library for these names. Most likely, it will cast no doubt on the fact that all of these men existed. Talk to your history teacher. He or she will likely recognize and affirm that history proves that these men existed and that the literature ascribed to them is reliable. Yet try to talk about the authority of the Bible based on the overwhelming amount of recent copies of original manuscripts, and he or she will likely find some way of explaining it away. Some adults simply believe what they choose to believe, even when the evidence points in the opposite direction of their "facts."

Your teenage friends at school, however, are a different story. They are not set in their ways and beliefs and are much more open to the truth of God's Word. True, they may need some questions answered, but if some of the logic and facts in this chapter are explained, they may indeed give the Bible a second look. By helping to establish its authority, you've broken down a barrier that prevents pre-Christians from allowing God to speak directly to them. Remember, it's not your job to *convince* anyone of anything. It's your job to be ready to defend the faith as best you can.

WHEN AND WHY WAS THE NEW TESTAMENT PUT TOGETHER IN THE FORM WE HAVE NOW?

In about A.D. 140, a heretic named Marcion developed his own Bible and began to preach from it. The church needed to offset his influence by determining what the real canon (measuring rod) of the New Testament Scripture was. Also, many Eastern church services were using books that were definitely not from authoritative sources.

It was decided that only manuscripts that could, without a doubt, be traced to those who lived when Christ lived (Peter, Paul, Matthew, John, James, Jude) or to those who had a close association with the apostles would be allowed to be called Scripture. (Luke is said to have written Luke and Acts under Paul's influence, and Mark wrote the book of Mark by copying down what Peter said.)

Athanasius of Alexandria (A.D. 367) gives us the earliest list of New Testament books that corresponds exactly to the books that make up our present New Testament.

HOW DID WE GET THE OLD TESTAMENT BIBLE?

Originally, it was passed down orally through men whose job it was to memorize what had been told to them by preceding generations; men whose entire purpose in life was to make sure that succeeding generations knew what God had done among their people. After language began to be written down using an alphabet (about the fifth century B.C.), the Scriptures were copied over and over by scribes. Because the climate caused the material onto which they copied the Scriptures—thin parchment (animal skins) and papyrus—to deteriorate over time, copying was a constant process.

Up until 285 B.C. the Old Testament Scriptures were all copied down in Hebrew or Aramaic. This period of history was dominated by Greek culture. Demetrius, the librarian for King Ptolemy of Alexandria (where the world's greatest library was located), had every book except a Greek version of (what we call) the Old Testament. Ptolemy enlisted seventy of his most educated scholars who knew Jewish law and could translate Hebrew and Aramaic into Greek. He asked each to translate the Old Testament Scriptures, working separately. After seveny-two days, the work was done—*and each translation corresponded exactly to the others!* This became known as the LXX (seventy), or the Septuagint.

Was the Septuagint an accurate copy of the Hebrew writings?

In 1947 thousands of parchments known collectively as the Dead Sea Scrolls were discovered in Israel. These fragments of the Old Testament have a date of about 125 B.C. Among the texts was nearly an entire copy of the book of Isaiah. Before this was discovered, the earliest existing copy of the book of Isaiah came from a scroll called the Masoretic (Hebrew) text. It is dated at A.D. 916—over one thousand years later. They are nearly the same, word for word! This shows the unusual accuracy of Scripture copying over a thousand-year period.

HOW DO ARCHAEOLOGICAL DISCOVERIES HELP PROVE THE BIBLE?

Josh McDowell says that "while archaeology can verify history and shed light on various passages of the Bible, it is beyond the realm of archaeology to prove the Bible is the Word of God."

Archaeology without historical record, however, is pointless. Digging up other people's trash and ruins only tells us of cultural customs and events. It doesn't give us the exact chronology of history (like the Bible does).

"What archaeology has done," says Josh, "is to verify some of the history contained in the Bible. For instance, two of the cities mentioned in the Bible, Sodom and Gomorrah, have been for many years considered mythological by the intellectual community. However, recent excavations at Tell Mardikh, now known to be the site of Ebla, uncovered about 15,000 tablets. Some of these have been translated, and mention is made of Sodom and Gomorrah.

ISN'T THE BIBLE FULL OF ERRORS?

You'll likely hear this one a lot in your lifetime. It is usually said by those who have never read the Bible and are simply looking for an excuse to stay in control of their own lives. But let's assume it's an honest question coming from a seeking heart. What does the Bible say about itself? Well, there are two passages you can refer to:

All Scripture is God-breathed and is useful for teaching, rebuking, correcting and training in righteousness, so that the man of God may be thoroughly equipped for every good work.
2 TIMOTHY 3:16–17

Above all, you must understand that no prophecy of Scripture came about by the prophet's own interpretation. For prophecy never had its origin in the will of man, but men spoke from God as they were carried along by the Holy Spirit.
2 PETER 1:20–21

The word "God-breathed" is a translation of the Greek word *theopneustos,* meaning inspired. Thus the origin of Scripture is God, not man; it is inspired.

For two hundred years, there has been a huge discussion among Christians as to whether these passages are saying that the Bible is "inerrant" (without errors) or simply "inspired." The first two words would make you believe that there are no contradictions in the Bible. In fact, there are several passages that *do* seem to be contradictory (see "Resolving 'Contradictions' in the Bible" at the end of this book). We tend to agree with Dr. Youngblood when he says, "I believe that the original writers' work was inerrant. Those copying it, however, were subject to the kinds of human errors even the most thorough and dedicated scribes can make."

Do the so-called "contradictions" change the overall message of the Bible? Hardly. In fact, any reasonable person would have to admit they do not detract from even the smallest messages of the Bible, let alone the major themes.

WHY IT IS DIFFICULT TO "PROVE" CHRISTIANITY TO YOUR FRIENDS BY USING THE BIBLE?

When Paul used the Old Testament Scriptures to persuade people about Jesus, he was talking to Jews, who were already convinced of the Scriptures' authority. From his example, is it possible to reasonably conclude that a friend at school should also have a high degree of respect for the Bible? If you quote it while making a case for a certain subject, should you automatically assume they should believe your argument just because it comes from the Bible?

The answer to both questions is no. Those outside the church will not have the same respect for the Bible that Christians do. That leaves you with a choice: you can arrogantly proceed to quote passages that "prove" you to be right, or you can meet these people where they are, and reasonably (and often slowly) move them toward checking out the Bible for themselves.

We (Mike and Greg) vote for the latter. Instead of using the truth of the Bible as a club, Christians all should hold it high and encourage seeking unbelievers to check things out for themselves. As that happens, the power of

God's Word can hit with full effect. When a heart and mind go one-on-one with the Holy Spirit through his Word, God *always* wins!

ON YOUR OWN

1. What does Jesus say about the Old Testament? Look up these passages and write down the significance of his words:
   - Matthew 5:17; 21:42; 26:54–56
   - Luke 24:25–27
   - John 5:39; 17:17

2. What importance does Jesus give to the Old Testament Scriptures?
   - Matthew 19:4–5
   - Mark 12:18–27

3. What do these passages say about the authority of Jesus?
   - Matthew 28:18
   - Mark 1:27
   - Mark 2:10–11

4. When the leaders of the early church talked to Jews and God-fearing Gentiles, how did they try to convince them?
   - Acts 17:2–4
   - Acts 17:11–12
   - Acts 18:28

5. When Paul talked to those who knew nothing about the Old Testament, how did he do it?
   - Acts 17:16–34
   - Acts 24:10–23

WITH A GROUP

1. Look up the passages above and answer the questions.

2. What do people at school think or say about the Bible?

3. What is it about the Bible that makes you sometimes doubt that it is actually God's Word?

4. What is it about the Bible that makes you realize that it really is God's Word?

5. What points would you use if someone asked you to prove whether the Bible is THE authority? Name your top three.

4

Popularity:
Is It Worth the Chase?

I s it wrong to be involved with outside activities or excel in school or have a close relationship to help make you feel you're worth something?

Not always, but it can be.

The next time you're walking through the hallways, look around. What you'll see are classmates involved in dozens of activities (drama, sports, rally, student government) or types of groups (science club, stoners, thrashers, Christians).

How would these people feel about themselves if their group or activity was somehow taken away from them? Some would be devastated. All they have in life is what they DO or what group they belong to.

What about you?

What if *your* abilities didn't measure up or all of your social groups suddenly left you in the dust? How would YOU feel?

Do you have anything inside that would tell you that you're still worthwhile, that you're not just one of five and a half billion people groping their way through life but a unique and special person who was created—for a reason—by a powerful, loving God?

Both Mike and I have known hundreds of Christian students who went to church but still pursued activities and friends that provided the IMMEDI-ATE — *though artificial* — rewards they thought they needed.

In a sense, they're Christian geeks, because they haven't grasped just WHO they actually are.

ULTIMATE GEEK RESPONSES

- When you start to feel like you don't fit in with the cool people at school, find out where the next Friday night party is and make an appearance. (Extra geek points: get drunk and make a fool of yourself so everyone will be talking about you Monday morning.)
- Realizing that smart people usually don't fit in with the cool crowd, quit studying for tests and don't work as hard in class. That way your grades will get worse and you can have cooler (though slightly less intelligent) friends.
- When a friend at school suddenly gets a bad reputation (like the label "geek"), act like a geek yourself by (1) avoiding him or her like the plague and (2) picking on him or her . . . right along with the crowd.
- Find only one group to hang with, and *never* associate with any other.

Christians have living inside of them the Creator of the universe; but in this area, they've left him standing just barely inside the door of their heart. Sadly, instead of allowing God to speak words of truth to them about how special, important, and unique they are, they pursue short-term feelings of self-worth by chasing popularity.

WHAT MAKES PEOPLE WORTHWHILE?

Ask someone you know that question and you'll get answers like this:

- a sense of humor
- good looks
- honesty
- a good personality
- athletic skills
- a supportive family
- trustworthiness
- money
- muscles
- a trim bod
- a high IQ
- a cool car

Some of this list makes sense, doesn't it? After all, you wouldn't want to spend time with someone who had a bad personality or who was dishonest. The things on this list may determine if someone is worthwhile to YOU, but does that mean that if people don't possess these things, they're not worthwhile? From the way some people are treated— and the way some people feel about themselves—you'd think so.

But it doesn't!

The reason?

But God demonstrates his own love for us in this:
While we were still sinners, Christ died for us.

ROMANS 5:8

If Jesus Christ died for all sinners (everyone), this means that each person has value to God. Not just the rich, the good-looking, the intelligent, the athletic, the popular —EVERYONE!

The obvious problem is that those who don't know Christ don't believe it. Do you know why? Because most *Christians* at your school don't believe it, either. It's easy to tell—they're simply acting like everyone else who doesn't know his or her own worth, and doing whatever it takes to be popular.

IT'S NOT ALL THEIR FAULT

Let's back off here for a moment. We don't want to be too hard on *every* Christian teen. Some honestly can't help the way they behave or how they feel about themselves. Here are a few of the main reasons:

Their family. If a girl grows up in a home in which her mother worried more about her daughter's *outward* appearance than about her *inward* character, that's likely what the girl will worry about most during her teen years.

If a guy is raised by a father trying to relive his adolescence through his son by pushing him toward sports from a very early age, the son is going to feel good about himself only if he's a good athlete who makes the team in every sport he plays.

If a girl is raised by critical parents who rarely encourage her—even if she only gets one B and the rest A's on her report card—she's going to feel like she has to perform at the top levels of academic excellence before her parents will show her love.

If a boy's dad works a lot or is gone from the home, the boy will rarely have the chance to see what a Christian man is supposed to act like. Consequently, he's going to make it up as he goes—and he's not always going to make the right decisions.

All of these situations happen in "good Christian homes." The result is that children don't realize they are loved unconditionally by God. Therefore they act accordingly, pursuing popularity or doing things that make them feel better about themselves.

The crowd. If you're not "playing the game" during your junior high and high school years, you're probably not popular. "Playing the game" is doing those things that are socially acceptable. Though the rules are different at each school—and in each part of the country—here are a few of the most familiar:

- dating popular classmates (or for girls, dating older guys)
- wearing the right clothes
- driving the right truck or car
- going to the right parties
- using the right "language" (swearing)
- having a loud stereo in your car
- not being friends with "nerds"

It's sad but true. Social survival at some schools is dependent on how you measure up in these areas. And if you don't measure up, you're not cool. And if you're not cool, what are you? You're a wannabe. You're trying to break into the cool crowd. And what happens if you can't break in? You feel bad about yourself. You feel like an outcast. You feel like you'll never have any "friends." (And believe it or not, some teens even resort to extreme behavior because they can't break in!)

There ARE those who don't play this game: students who don't care what anyone thinks. Sometimes they're Christians, sometimes they're not.

If there is one goal that Christian students should have during their teenage years, it's to feel secure in who God made them to be. Unfortunately, many are concerned with what the crowd thinks—and are spending every waking moment trying to figure out how to get in with the popular kids.

Most teens don't realize it, but the moment they graduate from high school, all of these people who were so important for so many years are suddenly ... gone! If you've spent your high school years "playing the game" to fit in, you'll likely keep doing it when you get to college. It's a sad way to live, but Christian teens are choosing this way in every school in America.

The popular culture. Believe it or not, millions of teens think that if they don't measure up to Hollywood's standards—either by looks, personality, or abilities—then they just can't compete. We'll deal more with this later, but it's obvious that TV, movies, and music groups are being used by the Father of Lies (Satan) to make teens not believe they are really worth something. Females are especially susceptible to comparing themselves to what girls' magazines tell them is the perfect girl.

What do people do when they don't like themselves because of what their family, their friends, or the popular culture has taught them?

Sadly, instead of finding out the truth—how much God values them just like they are—they do four things:

1. They attempt to NUMB themselves from the rejection they feel through alcohol, drugs, pornography, or overeating.

2. They try to ESCAPE the feelings of worthlessness through astrology, the occult, romance novels, movies, TV, or sometimes suicide.

3. They MASK their feelings of inadequacy through intellectualism, being the class clown, putting themselves down so others will pay attention to them, or being an overachiever in school in order to please teachers and parents (since they can't please their peers).

4. They IGNORE the rejection and try to please everyone; they put up a good front and in vain continue their attempts to get what they think they need: the approval of the crowd.

How can you listen and believe the quiet truth of what God thinks about you, when so many people are screaming in your ear lies straight from the pit of Hell?

First of all, you've got to want the truth more than the lies. A lot of Christian teens know exactly who they are in

> If your self-image is founded on misinformation, then your behavior and actions will be inaccurate.
>
> Definition of *self-image*: The accumulation of all the attitudes we have perceived about ourselves since birth.
>
> Definition of *self-esteem*: The corresponding feeling we have about this image of ourselves.

Christ, but they refuse to act accordingly, because popularity is a more immediate and tangible goal. Jesus said, "Then you will know the truth, and the truth will set you free" (John 8:32). Well, they know the truth, but they haven't allowed it to set them free.

God's not a yeller. Though he is constantly pursuing you, he prefers to do it in a quiet, subtle way. Satan, on the other hand, is a raving lunatic. He'll try anything to divert your attention away from the truth.

Second, if you're tired of the game and ready to allow God to speak words of truth to you, it's time to do something "unnatural." Sit down in the quietness of your room (no stereo, please), and let the invisible God speak the truth to you through his Word. The Bible isn't just for old people, parents, or pastors, it's for YOU! The only way you can *believe* the truth and *act on* the truth is to *know* the truth.

WHAT DOES GOD REALLY THINK OF YOU?

You've heard that God loves you. And you know that God allowed his Son, Jesus Christ, to die on a cross—and pay the penalty of your sin—to demonstrate the extent of that love. Then why don't more Christians act like this is the most incredible news we've ever heard? If God—the One who created us—says we are worthy of *his* love, why do we pursue what our culture thinks we should in order to feel good about ourselves?

We're immature, that's why!

We think the world revolves around us. And it takes a few years of really knowing the **right God** to realize that *he* is the center of the universe, not us.

Did you notice the emphasis on "right God"? Because of a weird upbringing or a bad church experience, many teens don't really know the right God. They may have different perceptions of who he is:

- He's a stern judge who's only interested in giving commandments to his people to keep them in line.
- He's like a heavenly Santa Claus, someone we turn to only when we want something.
- He's still a baby in a manger, not really strong enough to do anything.

The faster your eyes can focus on the *real* God through a relationship with Jesus Christ, the faster you'll not only believe but feel like you really have worth—just for being who he's created you to be.

Having an inability to relate to the right God and see yourself from his perspective isn't just a teenage disease, either. Adults often carry the same feelings of self-centeredness throughout their lives.

Let's make a quick distinction here: self-centeredness does not always equal selfishness. People can be caring and giving but still not feel worthwhile. Though they've learned how to be nice, they aren't viewing themselves the way God does.

So how can you begin seeing yourself the way God does?

- Read the Word and let the truth set you free from the pressure to please the crowd.
- Memorize a few passages that particularly stand out to you. (A number of passages in the "On Your Own" or "With a Group" sections would be a good start.)
- Hang with friends who tell you the truth—encouragers.
- Practice spotting lies when they come your way. If a teacher, parent, or friend calls you ignorant, recognize that that's not God's opinion.

How do you build others up?

- Tell them the truth about who they are. Be one of the few who remind their friends of their strengths and abilities.
- Making a few friendly putdowns often becomes a habit. Cut back on the cuts!
- Be a defender of your friends when they're in front of you or when someone is talking behind their backs.
- Point others to the One who will always tell them the truth.

Here's a good quote to remember: Treat people as they are, and they will remain that way. Treat them the way God would treat them, and you'll help them become what they were meant to be.

ON YOUR OWN

1. Read Psalm 139. Write down what the writer says about the way God looks at us.

2. Look up 2 Corinthians 10:12. What does comparing yourself to others tell about you?

3. According to these passages, how should we feel about our imperfections?

   ✎ 2 Corinthians 12:9

   ✎ Isaiah 45:9

   ✎ Romans 9:20

4. According to these passages, what shouldn't we be worrying about?

   ✎ Matthew 6:27–28

   ✎ Luke 12:15

   ✎ Philippians 4:4–9

5. According to these passages, what is God most concerned with?

   ✎ 1 Samuel 16:7

   ✎ Micah 6:8

   ✎ Matthew 23:23

WITH A GROUP

1. Do you like to give your opinion? Now's your chance. Circle whether you (A) agree or (D) disagree with the statements below.

   A D   Everyone has a need to be accepted by somebody.

   A D   To be really happy, a person must be liked by everyone.

A   D   People must prove they are worth being accepted before they can be.

A   D   Many people don't accept themselves.

A   D   Some people will do anything to be accepted.

A   D   Most things people do to try to earn acceptance backfire.

A   D   It's wrong to try to earn the acceptance of others.

A   D   Try as they might, some people can't find anyone to accept them.

A   D   To feel good about yourself, you need to be accepted by others.

A   D   It's important to realize that you are accepted by God.

Discuss each point and try not to be afraid to share what you believe.

2. Do you tend to concentrate more on your strengths or weaknesses? How about when you think of others: strengths or weaknesses?

3. According to these passages, what have you been given if you're a Christian?

   ✎ 1 Corinthians 2:16

   ✎ Ephesians 1:3

   ✎ 1 John 4:13

   ✎ Philippians 4:19

   ✎ Colossians 1:22

4. According to these passages, who are you if you have Christ?

   ✎ Ephesians 2:19

   ✎ 1 Corinthians 3:16

- ✎ John 1:12
- ✎ 1 Corinthians 12:27
- ✎ 2 Corinthians 5:17
5. Why has God created you?
   - ✎ Ephesians 2:8–10
   - ✎ 1 Corinthians 12:14–27
   - ✎ 1 Peter 2:9–10
   - ✎ Romans 12:1–2

5

Is It a Choice ... Or Is It a Child?

ANDY AND THE FIRING SQUAD

Andy Pottenger's heart was racing full throttle, and his stomach felt like a toxic waste dump.

The frantic sixteen-year-old was about to stand before the firing squad in fifth-period speech—and attempt to say something intelligent.

His assignment: Go head-to-head with another student and debate abortion. Andy would make a pro-life case in favor of unborn babies.

His opponent: Nicole Swan, Central High's student body president (gorgeous, popular, voted "most likely to succeed," a straight-A student, *and*—GULP!—a convincing speaker).

Andy had a reputation for being pro-life, ever since a news crew filmed him and his youth group praying outside an abortion clinic. But when his speech teacher insisted his final project be a debate, Andy came down with a major case of the jitters.

I'm NO EXPERT! he thought. *What on earth have I gotten myself into?!*

KELLIE'S HISTORY LESSON

Kellie scrunched into a tiny ball and rested her chin on her knee. The conversation between her history study partners was almost too much to handle.

"Are you sure, Holly?" Danielle pressed. "I mean, you could be a little late because of midterms ... stress, stuff like that."

"Look, I'm not just *a little* late. Trust me, I know what's happening inside my own body." Holly put her hand on her stomach and looked down. "I'm about fourteen weeks along."

"Have you told your parents?" Melanie asked.

"Are you kidding?! They'd freak."

"How about ... him?" Danielle added.

Holly shook her head. "No."

A stabbing pain shot through Kellie's stomach as she listened. As a Christian, she couldn't imagine facing such a hard dilemma. But what she heard next nearly made her blood boil.

"We have a health clinic right here on campus," Danielle said. "They can tell you where to go to—you know—take care of it."

"And they WON'T tell your parents," Melanie said.

"I heard it's a pretty simple procedure," Danielle added. "They remove a bunch of cells and tissue ... and in five minutes, it's over."

Kellie sat up and gulped. *It's a child,* she thought, *not a wart. They want to vacuum up a human like a piece of trash!*

"Did you have something to add?" Danielle asked, looking right at Kellie.

"Yeah, you've been so quiet. Speak up!" Melanie barked.

Kellie looked at Holly and swallowed. "Well, uhhh . . . I just feel that . . . "

What can I say . . . without them thinking that I'm some kinda religious geek? I KNOW what I feel inside—I just can't put it into words.

Notice how life is full of certain touchy topics? Super-sensitive subjects that generate explosions of volcanic emotion . . . endless arguments . . . warring camps.

Abortion is one of them.

Some say we should define human life by age, believing that the bulge in a mom's stomach isn't really a baby but "fetal tissue." Does this mean that if people are too old, it's okay to get rid of them too?

Some say we should make sure that all babies are "normal" before they're considered human (we should abort those with Down's syndrome, for example). Does this mean babies with genetic deformities (like sickle-cell anemia) can be declared nonhuman?

Some say you have to be wanted by someone be-

> "It's interesting to note . . . that a woman who plans to terminate a pregnancy usually refers to the life within her as 'the fetus.' But if she intends to deliver and love and care for the little child, she affectionately calls him 'my baby.' The need for this distinction is obvious: If we are going to kill a human being without experiencing guilt, we must first strip it of worth and dignity. We must give it a clinical name that denies its personhood."
>
> DR. JAMES DOBSON

fore you qualify for membership in the human race. Do we then search the country and wipe out the people no one wants—such as AIDS victims or child abusers?

Let's assume you're convinced that abortion is (a) illogical or (b) scripturally wrong. What in the world can you do about it? How do you lead your friends in the right direction . . . and exactly what do you say?

ULTIMATE GEEK RESPONSES

- "You call yourself 'pro-choice'?! Gimme a break! You people are nothing but MURDERERS . . . baby killers . . . heartless spawn of Satan!"
- "Uhhh . . . I haven't yet formed an opinion about abortion. Sure, I'm a Christian—and my pastor says it's wrong—but I just don't know. I think there are plenty of good arguments on both sides. So I guess I'm kinda 'middle of the road.'"
- "Personally, I'm against abortion . . . but just do whatever *you* think is best. Hey, I won't step on your toes with *my* values."

A BETTER RESPONSE

The key is to defuse the bomb (human emotion) and present the facts. Impossible? Not if you:

- know what you believe and *why* you believe it
- don't argue but instead stay calm and confidently reveal the truth
- dispel the myths and show how many proabortion arguments are manipulative, unreasonable, and callous to the truth

Let's sit in on Andy's big speech to see if he's able to turn the tide of "politically correct" proabortion hype.

THE CLASSROOM DEBATE

Nicole kicked off the action, blasting away with several popular arguments for abortion.

> "If the baby has no right to be born, he can't have the right to housing, a job, or education. If we can't protect that right, all other rights are meaningless."
>
> KAY JAMES, DEPARTMENT OF HEALTH AND HUMAN SERVICES, VIRGINIA

"A woman has the right to privacy over her own body," she insisted. "NO ONE should ever take that away. What happens in a clinic is solely the business of a woman and her doctor."

Nicole paused, tossed back her long brunette hair, then locked eyes with Andy. *Just what are those antiabortionists trying to prove, anyway?*

"They distort the truth and tug at our emotions," she added. "They show us ghastly photos of nonbreathing fetuses in buckets and try to make the pro-choice side look like heartless butchers."

A few howls rose from the class. Andy slid down in his seat and nervously fumbled through his notes. *I'm definitely lunchmeat!* he thought, panicking.

"An abortion is a safe and simple medical procedure that doesn't murder a baby," Nicole continued. "It merely puts an end to an unwanted pregnancy."

"Let's review the facts...."

Without even looking at her notes, Nicole then launched into her speech:

"The fetus is an extension of the pregnant woman's body, like her teeth or tonsils.

"Since the unborn is nothing more than a bunch of tissue, abortion ends a pregnancy. It doesn't kill a baby.

"The fetus isn't yet a complete human being. It's more like a blueprint for a potential baby, not an actual one.

"Life begins at birth. That's why we celebrate birthdays, not conception days.

"Every woman has a right to reproductive freedom, especially control over her own body. That's why we must preserve our right to choose.

"If abortion is made illegal, thousands of women will lose their lives to rusty clothes hangers in back alleys.

"The unborn isn't a person with meaningful life. It can't even think and is less advanced than an animal.

"It's wrong to bring an unwanted baby into this world. The child will probably end up unloved and abandoned."

Nicole's final punch

After walking the class through these key pro-choice points, Nicole pulled out the heavy artillery ... and ended her speech with a jolt: "What about a woman whose unborn baby is diagnosed as being deformed or handicapped?" she asked. "What about a woman who is pregnant due to rape or incest? Isn't it more cruel to force her to have the baby than to end the pregnancy ... and erase the horrible memory?

"That radical minority that calls itself pro-life can't shove their religious beliefs down our throats," Nicole concluded. "And we can't let them step all over our right to free choice."

> "If we accept that a mother can kill even her own child, how can we tell other people not to kill each other? ... Any country that accepts abortion is not teaching its people to love but to use any violence to get what they want."
>
> MOTHER TERESA

The room thundered with applause. Nearly everyone clapped and howled their support.

Nicole walked past Andy and smiled. "Good luck, Pottenger ... you'll need it!"

A den of lions

It was Andy's turn now, and it was almost as if fifth-period speech had transformed from a safe classroom to a dangerous jungle—filled with fierce predators.

As he looked out at his classmates, the football-sized hands of the school's quarterback, who was sitting in the front row, suddenly looked more like the deadly paws of a husky lion. Even the teacher's tall, fluffy beehive resembled the matted mane of the king of beasts.

Andy swallowed and squeezed his eyes shut. *Lord, they're gonna pounce on every word and chew up every idea,* he prayed silently. *I'm in a den of lions … HELP!*

> ### A Reason to Abort?
> One doctor said to another, "I would like your opinion about the termination of a pregnancy. The father has syphilis. The mother has tuberculosis. Of their first four children born, the first was blind, the second died, the third was deaf and dumb, the fourth was also tuberculous. What would you have done?"
>
> "I would have ended the pregnancy," said the second doctor.
>
> "Then you would have murdered Beethoven."
>
> P. B. MEDAWAR,
> *LIFE OR DEATH: ETHICS AND OPTIONS*

"And now, class, we'll hear an *anti*abortion argument from Andy Pottenger," the teacher announced.

Andy took his place behind the podium and scanned the crowded classroom. His knees shook and his mouth felt like it was full of peanut butter. But he tried to concentrate on all the stuff his youth pastor had taught him … and all the spine-chilling photos he had seen.

It's up to me to set the facts straight, he thought.

Truth is truth

"Nicole bombarded us with point after point about women's rights and free choice," Andy said. "But she completely missed what's *really* at stake: a living, functioning HUMAN LIFE."

A few groans rose from the crowd. Andy gripped the podium and focused on his notes. "Abortionists blast pro-lifers for showing photos of dead babies in buckets, claiming we're distorting fact with cheap theatrics.

"But truth is truth: *dead babies who are discarded is exactly what abortion amounts to. Every abortion stops a beating heart.*"

"Let's review the facts. . . ."

Andy's last statement made a few heads pop up, but he knew he faced an uphill battle. So he stepped to the side of the podium and tried to make eye contact with each kid in class as he continued his speech:

"*A fetus is NOT just another part of a woman's body.* A body part is defined by the common genetic code it shares with the rest of its body. The unborn's genetic code differs from the mother's, even to the extent that some unborn babies are male, while their moms are female.

"*An unborn human is NOT just a blob of tissue.* From the moment of conception, the unborn *is* what it *is* . . . a separate, LIVING human being. At six weeks, you can see a beating heart. At twelve weeks, eyes and hands can be observed.

"*A fetus is NOT just a blueprint or a potential human.* A fetus is a person at a particular stage of development—much like a toddler or an adolescent. The fact is, something non-human does not become human by getting older and bigger.

"*Life does NOT begin at birth.* Science has shown us that human life begins at conception. All genetic characteristics of a distinct individual are present from the

Gruesome Stats

- Thirty-one million abortions have been performed in the U.S. since 1973.
- By the time you finish reading this chapter, thirty babies will have been aborted. An abortion is performed in this country every twenty seconds—an estimated forty-three hundred per day.
- Nearly two hundred thousand second- and third-trimester abortions are performed annually—seventeen thousand of those occur after five months of pregnancy.
- Nearly half of all women obtaining abortions admit to not using any method of birth control during the month that they became pregnant.
- The abortion industry is a business that is estimated to generate four hundred million dollars a year.

How Abortions Are Done

Suction aspiration. Ninety percent of all abortions involve the use of a high-powered vacuum that is inserted in the womb. Its purpose is to suck the baby out into a container so it can be dumped.

Dilation and curettage. Here a loop-shaped knife is inserted to cut the baby apart; the pieces are scraped out through the cervix.

Dilation and evacuation. A grasping forceps (similar to pliers with teeth) is inserted into the womb to tear apart the baby one piece at a time.

Saline injection. A concentrated salt solution is injected into the womb. The baby swallows the solution and usually dies one to two hours later from burned-out lungs, dehydration, brain hemorrhaging, and convulsions.

moment of conception. Our recognition of birthdays is cultural, not scientific.

"*Denying abortion does NOT step all over a woman's rights and freedoms.* The one-time choice of abortion robs someone else of a lifetime of choices and creates pain for the mother, not to mention others involved. Furthermore, responsible societies *must* deny choices that would harm others.

"*If abortion is made illegal, thousands of women will NOT die from rusty clothes hangers.* Prior to its legalization, ninety percent of abortions were done not in back alleys but by physicians in their offices. In fact, women in America still die from *legal* abortions.

"*The early stage of human life IS as meaningful as any other stage.* But if we listened to abortionists, who base human value on size and intelligence, then we'd also have to dehumanize other members of society: dwarfs, basketball centers, the obese, the mentally handicapped. And when we dehumanize the beginning of life, we dehumanize the end of it as well.

"*Since human life IS valuable, every human IS wanted.* A pregnancy may be unwanted, but there is no such thing as an unwanted child. The list of couples wanting to adopt runs into the millions. And if we destroy all human beings we believe are 'unwanted,' then *any* segment of society is at risk: AIDS victims, the elderly, derelicts, et cetera."

Andy's final punch

"Using phrases like 'terminating a pregnancy' may sound better, but the fact is that *abortion IS deadly*. EVERY abortion stops a beating heart and terminates measurable brain waves."

The entire class sat perfectly still. The snide smirks and rolling eyes had turned to blank stares. Nicole looked bored ... and occasionally glanced out the window or scribbled little circles on her algebra book cover.

Andy stepped away from the podium and delivered *his* knockout blow: "Americans kill nearly one and a half million unborn babies a year through abortion," he explained. "That's more than four thousand a day, or one about every twenty seconds.

"Hitler killed six million Jews," Andy continued. "But since 1973, Americans have exterminated more than thirty-one million unborn babies. No matter what some believe, the truth is that abortion kills . . . *and that's wrong.*"

As Andy closed, the fierce lions in fifth-period speech began to look a lot more like purring house cats. But even if he hadn't changed everyone's mind, Andy had set the facts straight . . . and had done his part to geek-proof the pro-life cause!

ON YOUR OWN

1. Think about it. Doctors say that just twenty-eight days after conception, a half-inch long human fetus has a developing brain as well as a beating heart. With this in mind, check out Psalm 139:13, 15–16.

2. Now complete the following:

   ✎ Psalm 139 makes it clear that a fetus is not simply "a mass of tissue" or a "potential life," because . . .

   ✎ Abortion is not an option for Christians, because . . .

3. List three things that are unique about you (talents, abilities, strengths).

   ✎

   ✎

   ✎

4. For a moment, imagine that you had been aborted. If you weren't in the picture today, how would your family be different? What would your friends be like? (Think of some ways in which your life has impacted the lives of others.)

5. Read 1 Corinthians 6:19–20. Based on this passage, answer the following:

   ✎ Has God given us absolute ownership of our bodies?

   ✎ How does this Scripture passage affect the argument that a woman should have "control over her body" and "the right to choose abortion"?

WITH A GROUP

1. Some proabortion Christians claim that since the Bible does not specifically condemn it, abortion must not be wrong. Take a look at these Scripture passages: Job 31:15, Jeremiah 1:4–5, Luke 1:44 and Psalm 139:13.

   ✎ When does human life begin, at conception or at birth?

   ✎ What do the Scriptures say about the sanctity of human life?

   ✎ Is abortion murder?

2. You may have heard an argument that goes something like this: "The preborn are not fully human. Therefore it's not morally wrong to terminate a 'potential life.'" Check out Isaiah 49:1, Jeremiah 1:5, and Judges 13:3, 6–7.

   ✎ What do these passages say about the humanity of the preborn?

   ✎ Based on these Scripture passages—as well as the information presented in this chapter—do

humans become individuals at conception or
at birth?

3. Read Job 12:10. If God is the Author of Life,
   can abortion ever be an option? Can you cite
   a situation in which you think abortion might
   be okay?

4. Let's plunge ahead ten years into the future.
   Suppose this happens:

   ✎ You and your spouse are sitting in a doctor's
   office. The physician leans forward and looks
   you directly in the eye. "I have bad news. Your
   child is otherwise healthy, but our tests show
   that it hasn't developed legs or a right arm.
   And there's a chance it could be brain-
   damaged. If you wish, we can terminate the
   pregnancy right now."

   ✎ How would you react? What would you do?

Many concepts for this chapter were drawn from the book
Prolife Answers to Prochoice Arguments by Randy Alcorn; Mult-
nomah books, Questar Publishers; copyright 1992 by Randy
Alcorn.

6

Taking God to McDonald's

o you remember playing the "What-if" game when you were a kid? Here are three "What-if" situations you need to finish:

THE MISSING MONEY

After a few weeks of being trained by the manager, you were trusted to be on your own as a cashier at a fast-food place. One day, your till turned up ten dollars short at the end of your shift. The rule was that your pay was reduced by whatever shortage your register had (when the cash in your register was compared to the amount of sales you rang up).

You told your manager that you were certain you hadn't made any mistakes. Then you remembered a phone call that you had wanted to make about halfway through your shift. Another employee (who had been known for making mistakes in giving change) had been left alone out front where both registers were.

Here are possible steps you could take to make things right. Write down a number next to each step to indicate what you would try first, second, and so on. Cross out those things you wouldn't do.

_____ Tell the manager that in two months, you've never made a mistake, that you didn't give anyone too much change, that you're honest and didn't take the money, and that it's just not fair that you should be penalized for something you didn't do.

_____ Ask the other employee if she used your register. If so, ask whether she made any mistakes on it.

_____ Talk to your parents later and ask them to call the manager to try to convince her of how responsible you are and that it was probably another employee who made the mistake and then blamed it on you.

_____ The next time you work with that employee, take ten dollars out of her register while she's not around. That will make things even.

_____ Even though you know that it wasn't your fault, take responsibility for the missing ten dollars, learn from it (lock your register next time), and forget about it.

_____ Have the manager confront the other employee to see if she can intimidate her into admitting what happened.

_____ Quit.

_____ Ask never to work with that employee again.

_____ Admit that you could have made a mistake and take the deduction without arguing or complaining.

_____ Other:

WAL-MART SCAM

During the Christmas rush, you land a temporary four-to-nine job at Wal-Mart helping to keep the stockroom in order. The regular employees seem to be nice, and you make friends right away with a few guys your age. Since this is only your second real job, you not only want to perform well, you want to fit in with everyone else. Most of the guys you work with are older and out of high school. A couple of them take you under their wing and show you the ropes.

Your third Thursday night on the job, after your shift, Larry and Troy motion you over to where they're finishing up a task. As you walk over, Troy says he'll watch around the corner and walks past you.

"Hey Pete, do you have a CD player?" Larry asks.

"No, but I asked for one for Christmas. I'm not going to hold my breath, though. My parents are broke."

"Well, you don't have to wait for Christmas. Here, grab one of these Sony portables and stuff it in your pants."

"You want me to take a brand-new CD player?!"

"Hey, you're not stealing it. This whole box is going to be shipped back to the big Wal-Mart warehouse. It's full of Sony stuff that was returned for one reason or another. Wal-Mart sends it back to the Sony distributor and will get new stuff in return. We heard that when a box gets returned to Sony, they don't even check what's in it. They just look at what's on the list, and ship new stuff to Wal-Mart. The box probably gets tossed or something. So you see, it's not stealing. Just consider it a Christmas bonus from Wal-Mart for a job well done. Do you know how many *billions* of dollars they made last year? I don't think they're going to care what happens to a few CD players that cost five dollars to make in Japan."

"If they don't care, then why should I stuff it in my pants?"

"Look, I'm just trying to do you a favor. Do you want the CD player or not?"

"Well . . ."

Here are possible things you could say and do. Write down a number next to each to indicate what you would try first, second, and so on. Cross out those things you wouldn't do.

_____ Take the CD player, but return it later when the guys aren't around.

_____ Tell Larry, "Thanks, but no thanks. I don't have any CDs to play in it, anyway."

_____ Look Larry in the eye. Tell him that what he's doing is wrong and threaten to inform the supervisor about what's going on.

_____ Say, "No, thanks." Then walk away. The next day, tell the supervisor about what's going on.

_____ Figure that God is trying to bless and reward you for all of your hard work; take the CD player and say thanks to Larry.

_____ Ask Larry if you can have a day to think about it. The next day at school, talk to a couple of your Christian friends and ask their advice. After school, tell your mom about a "hypothetical situation" and get her opinion.

_____ Other:

BREAK ROOM CONFRONTATION

You've been bagging groceries at Safeway for about a month. You work the six-to-ten shift three nights a week, and then you work all day on Saturdays. The store manager has asked you to work Sundays, but you've told him you'd rather not because you go to church and want to spend time with your family. He hasn't forced you to work Sundays yet, though you can tell he hasn't been too happy about being turned down. He's even said, "The way to move up here at Safeway is to agree to any hours the manager gives you."

One Saturday afternoon, about two o'clock, you're taking your thirty-minute lunch in the break room. Because it's a slow time of day, there are about eight people in there. The conversation moves to what everyone is going to do on Sunday. Mabel, one of the older ladies, mentions that after church, she and her family are going out to the lake for a picnic. Two of the younger checkout ladies laugh and agree they won't be in ANY shape to be getting up before noon tomorrow morning.

One of the managers says that he wouldn't be caught dead in church, that it's too full of hypocrites. He goes on to tell a story of a pastor he once knew who divorced his wife and ran off with his secretary.

That starts the flow of complaints about church. One of the young checkout ladies says she used to go but they always talked too much about hell. "I thought church was a place where people were supposed to love each other. All I ever felt there was judgment."

A bagger friend you work with says he can't believe people actually would want to follow an old, hard-to-read book and some dead Jewish guy.

Another mentions that church plays an important role in society. "If we didn't have churches, where would people get married? And where would we have funerals? Besides, some people need a crutch to lean on, because they're not emotionally strong enough to make it alone. It provides them with friends who are like them."

Mabel finally speaks up. "I just think you've all had bad experiences. Church isn't like that at all. Forty years ago I heard that Jesus Christ loved me enough to die for my sins so I could go to heaven. Since I knew I wasn't perfect— and I wanted to go to heaven—I accepted him into my life. Church helps me learn more about God. It also provides a place where I can help others. Helping others—that's what church is all about."

"Help others ... right!" the store manager says. "Is that why my dad's church, which he went to for twenty years, helped me out of $150 to have his funeral there?" Suddenly he looks at you. "Hey, you go to church every week. Why would a young guy like you want to go? Or do your parents force you?"

"Ummm ..."

Again, here are some possible things you could say or do. Write down numbers next to each to indicate what you would try first, second, and so on. Cross out those things you wouldn't do.

_____ "Yeah, my parents have to make me go. But some-times I like it."

_____ "We've been going my whole life. I've never really thought about not going. It's just something our family does."

_____ "Whoa, look at the time. I'd better get back to work."

_____ "I agree with Mabel. Church is somewhere I go to learn more about God. Even though I'm only a teenager, I can still see that life is too tough to try to make it as the Lone Ranger. I really need church."

_____ Instead of saying anything about what you believe, repeat what everyone else has said. As you walk out, say, "Everyone's entitled to his or her own opinion."

_____ "Not everything about church is wonderful. There are hypocrites who attend. I suppose that's because Christians aren't perfect, they're human. So far, I haven't had too many bad experiences with it, and sometimes I even enjoy it."

_____ Other:

WHY SPEAK UP?

All three of these stories are examples of real-life dilemmas you'll face once you join the workforce. The first was a *Christian-character dilemma*. Will you, with the right attitude, take responsibility for something, or will you do anything to prove you were right?

The second was a *moral dilemma*. When confronted with the opportunity to do something you know is wrong—and regardless of whether you'll get caught or not—what will you do or say?

The third is a *courage dilemma*. Do you have the strength to stick up for Jesus Christ in the face of opposition, or will you deflate when the pressure hits?

How do you know what the right thing to say and do is without looking like a wishy-washy Christian geek? All three examples illustrate this one truth: **knowing** the right thing and **doing** it isn't easy!

If we knew there wouldn't be any social (or sometimes economic) consequences for our attempts to represent the Christian faith, most of us would know the right actions to take or words to speak. Ahhh, but sometimes there *are* consequences, aren't there? So we keep silent or say something that betrays what we know to be true. In the process, we feel guilty or stupid. What's the answer?

Well, that depends. How badly do you want to do the right thing? If you're satisfied with being a chameleon (you remember, that little animal that changes skin color to blend in with its surroundings), probably no amount of coaching or convincing will give you the courage to do something you don't want to do.

But let's assume you WANT to be more prepared. If that's the case, here are a few ideas on how to keep firm when your knees are weak.

Rehearse. With a parent, friend, or youth leader, go through as many situations as you can think of that could cause you to do the wrong thing. If you know what to expect and what to say—*before* it happens—you'll be much more confident.

But in your hearts set apart Christ as Lord. Always be prepared to give an answer to everyone who asks you to give the reason for the hope that you have. But do this with gentleness and respect, keeping a clear conscience, so that those who speak maliciously against your good behavior in Christ may be ashamed of their slander.

1 PETER 3:15–16

Get the word out. Unfortunately, many Christians want to be full-time in God's Secret Service. That is, they want the benefits of being a Christian, but they don't want anyone else to know they are one. You don't have to hand out tracts to inform your coworkers of your allegiance to Christ, but you can drop signals—low-key or high-octane, whatever you're comfortable with—to let them know where you stand. Here are a few examples of things to do or say:

- "Does your family have any Christmas (or Easter) traditions? We go to church on Christmas Eve and . . ."
- Read a pocket Bible or a Christian book on your break.
- "I've got to tell you about this Christian camp I went to last summer. You won't believe some of the things we did."
- Pray before inhaling your lunch.
- When someone mentions a struggle they're going through, let them know you'll pray for them. How? A short note or quick word is often all it takes.

I am not ashamed of the gospel, because it is the power of God for the salvation of everyone who believes: first for the Jew, then for the Gentile.

ROMANS 1:16

Let your actions speak loudly. At work, your job comes first. If you're not a good employee, you may end up giving all Christians a bad name. You're not a slave, but this verse applies nonetheless:

Slaves, obey your earthly masters in everything; and do it, not only when their eye is on you and to win their favor, but with sincerity of heart and reverence for the Lord.

COLOSSIANS 3:22

Don't bad-mouth your bosses behind their backs. It's true that nearly every employee ranks on his or her boss occasionally. So be unique and don't join in. That alone will show people there's something different about you.

Remind the people to be subject to rulers and authorities, to be obedient, to be ready to do whatever is good, to slander no one, to be peaceable and considerate, and to show true humility toward all men.

TITUS 3:1–2

Hold your tongue. When other workers start telling off-color jokes or making crude remarks, fight the urge to participate. Don't act superior or judgmental (after all, non-Christians *will* act like non-Christians), just try to keep quiet or turn away. Yes, this may mean that it will take longer to be included in the "group," but in the long run, what type of reputation do you want: a sheep who'll blend in with the gang because it's the safe thing to do, or a person of character who has a firm moral foundation?

Do not let any unwholesome talk come out of your mouths, but only what is helpful for building others up according to their needs, that it may benefit those who listen. . . . Nor should there be obscenity, foolish talk or coarse joking, which are out of place, but rather thanksgiving.

EPHESIANS 4:29; 5:4

TOUGH QUESTIONS

What's more important, the job or my faith?

When you are employed, the big-picture issue isn't how to earn a few bucks to help your parents with your car insurance, it's how to be God's man or woman in a particular place at a particular time. He has strategically placed you in a job not just to pad your bank account but to represent him to lost souls who (a) may have *never* been prayed for in their entire lives and therefore need you to fight for them on your knees, and (b) need you to move them up one more notch toward a faith in Christ. It's not your responsibility to save them (it's God's), but rather to be faithful and consistent in your beliefs as best you can, and to be ready to answer—or find the answers to—their questions.

All this is from God, who reconciled us to himself through Christ and gave us the ministry of reconciliation ... And he has committed to us the message of reconciliation. We are therefore Christ's ambassadors, as though God were making his appeal through us.

2 CORINTHIANS 5:18–20

What if my boss asks me to do something that I know is wrong?

While this question seems like a no-brainer, Christians will often obey their bosses instead of their consciences. Whether it's filling out your time card differently to prevent your boss from having to do more paperwork, or cutting corners to give the appearance that the job is complete, or telling a white lie to your boss's boss so that your boss doesn't get into trouble—the temptation to fudge on the truth needs to be fought off. Again, it may mean you'll have to take some grief for not "going along," but the big picture must be kept in mind.

People are watching. And though you may not score any points with your boss, a coworker may need to observe strong convictions in action before they decide they want such convictions for themselves (even a co-worker not warm to Christianity). That which could help bring another to faith in Christ just may be you getting fired or demoted because you did what was right. You decide. Which is more important?

But even if you should suffer for what is right, you are blessed. . . . It is better, if it is God's will, to suffer for doing good than for doing evil.

1 PETER 3:14, 17

What should I do if my boss chews me out in front of everyone?

Sadly, some bosses abuse the authority they've been given. They feel it necessary to put employees "in their place" in front of others in order to set an example of what could happen to the other employees if they mess up. It's a poor way to manage, and actually does more harm than good. A boss needs to have the respect of his or her workers in order for them to function efficiently. Tirades rarely cause workers to respect their boss.

The key issue here isn't whether you deserve the tongue-lashing or not, it's your response to the episode. If you can respond patiently and respectfully (even with someone who doesn't deserve it), others will notice. And if they notice, they just might wonder where your inner strength comes from.

If you *did* mess up, take the medicine that is handed out. Apologize if your boss lets you, explain your side if your boss asks you to, but accept responsibility for your actions. Don't blame it on anyone else.

If you *didn't* mess up, yet you're getting chewed on anyway—again, take it. Defend yourself in a respectful way if you have the chance, both in front of your coworkers and in private. But when it's all over, fight the urge to get back at or bad-mouth your boss later. Nobody wins when that happens, and you might lose the credibility you've been building up with your coworkers.

When they hurled their insults at him, he [Jesus] did not retaliate; when he suffered, he made no threats. Instead, he entrusted himself to him who judges justly.

1 PETER 2:23

What if I see a health hazard that's being ignored?

Always report it. If your immediate boss won't listen, call or write a note (anonymously, if you must) to his or her boss and inform them about what's happening. Keeping silent is never your best option.

ON YOUR OWN

1. Look up these passages and apply them to your situation. What are you *really* responsible to do?

   ✎ Romans 15:18

   ✎ Romans 10:1

   ✎ 1 Corinthians 3:6–11

   ✎ 1 Corinthians 5:9–11

   ✎ Ephesians 5:15–16

   ✎ Colossians 1:28–29

2. What do these passages tell you about what Paul's ultimate goal was? How would he benefit by pursuing that goal?

   ✎ 1 Corinthians 9:16–23

   ✎ 2 Corinthians 6:3

   ✎ 1 Corinthians 10:32–33

3. According to these passages, what are we really fighting against?

   ✎ 2 Corinthians 4:4

   ✎ Ephesians 4:18

   ✎ Ephesians 6:11–12

4. How do these passages relate to being a Christian in the marketplace?

   ✎ Philippians 2:4

   ✎ Ephesians 6:7

   ✎ Colossians 4:5–6

5. How should you respond if coworkers say you're just a kid?

   ✎ 1 Timothy 4:12–16

   ✎ 2 Timothy 4:2–5

WITH A GROUP

1. What other situations arise in which a Christian is tempted to compromise his or her faith or give in to pressure from co-workers?

2. How does God use our bad circumstances to help others? (See 2 Corinthians 1:3–7.)

3. Can you think of any examples in which God has used your bad times to help others?

4. What will be the consequences for someone if they live their entire life separated from God? (See 2 Thessalonians 1:8–10, Hebrews 9:27, 2 Peter 3:9.)

5. What should you do when you are tempted to give up?
    - ✎ Galatians 6:9
    - ✎ Hebrews 12:3
    - ✎ Revelation 2:10

7

Looking Forward to Sex ...
When It's <u>Really</u> Safe

DUSTIN IN THE LOCKER ROOM

"She's an absolute ten!" Matt says as he pulls off his practice jersey. He flings it into his locker, then pelts Dustin with a sweaty sock. "And she's going with a dweeb like YOU!"

"Unreal," Chris chimes in. "If I dated her ... ooohhh, dude ..." He falls to the floor, clutching his chest—faking a massive coronary.

Jesse slaps Dustin on the back and grins. "So ... you've been going out with her for three weeks, huh?! Just what happens when you two are alone—*totally alone?*"

Dustin shrugs. "You know ... stuff. We talk, watch TV ..."

"*And* ..." Jesse presses.

"Eat, study, talk some more ..."

The guys bomb Dustin—PLOP! THUD! SMACK!—with crusted gym clothes. Then Matt launches the ultimate question. "'Fess up, dude. Has she let you have it yet?"

Dustin looks up and swallows, sirens blazing in his head: GEEK ALERT—COOLNESS ABOUT TO BE CLOBBERED!

"Ahhh ... have what?" he asks nonchalantly, knowing full well which "it" his friend is referring to.

"IT, you idiot!" Matt barks. "Whaddaya think?"

Of course Dustin has never done it, and he isn't going to—until marriage. In his eyes, to move too fast too soon spells major headaches: pregnancy, sexual diseases, AIDS, broken hearts. And as a Christian, he has even better reasons to wait.

But the guys. . . . How on earth can he explain this to them?

Dustin looks Matt in the eye. "And I suppose you have?!"

Matt bristles. "Hey, think I'm gay?" he fires back. "'Course I've done it ... lots of times. What *normal* guy hasn't?"

Dustin's stomach knots up. He hates locker-room talk—especially when his reputation is on the line. He doesn't want to lie, BUT ...

"Well ... ahhh ..." Dustin pauses. "Actually, I ... I mean *we* ... ummm ..." (Inside, his geek alert suddenly reaches MEGACRITICAL status.)

What do I tell them? he wonders as he frantically searches for the precise words. *How do I stand for what's right, without being laughed at ... and without looking like a total geek?*

JAMIE HOME ALONE

"BRAD PURCELL!" Amber's voice screams through the phone. "You are absolutely the luckiest girl alive, Jamie Richards."

"It's too cool to believe," Jamie giggles, flopping down on her bed. "It's like an incredible dream, and I don't ever want to wake up. He actually asked me!"

"Amazing! The high school hunk of the century, and he asks *you* to be his girl," Amber sighs.

Jamie presses the receiver to her ear with her shoulder and leans back on her large stuffed Pink Panther doll. She begins to draw little hearts on her algebra book cover.

"How does this sound: Jamie and Brad . . . forever!"

"You dweeb!" Amber laughs. "That's what you said about Sean Mitchell."

"Ooooh . . . don't even mention him," Jamie says. "He was all hands and only had *one* thing on his mind. Brad, well, he's different."

"Earth to Jamie," Amber fires back. "As if I have to remind you, Brad is a guy—*a gorgeous guy!* And *all* guys have only one thing on their mind."

"Whatever, Amber."

"Look, Miss Church Lady," Amber says with that sarcastic tone Jamie hates, "you're not in kindergarten anymore. It's time you grew up a little. Maybe then guys wouldn't dump you so quickly."

Jamie stares at the ceiling in disgust. *Not THIS conversation again. When will Amber get the hint? I'm not that kind of girl.*

"Hey, did you know that my parents went away for the weekend?" Jamie says, hoping to change the subject.

"So you're home *alone*?!"

"Yep, the house is mine," Jamie says. "But my parents did leave behind a one-hundred-page list of rules. At the very top is NO GUYS ALLOWED!"

"That's perfect!" Amber says.

"Amber, what are you talking about?"

"Jamie, this is your chance. Your parents will never find out."

"Find out what?" Jamie says, deciding to play dumb.

"That you had a secret visitor. And that you and Brad—"

"Forget it, Amber. They'd know," Jamie says. "Believe me, they have their ways. Besides, I just don't . . . I mean, I'd never let a boy—"

"Go all the way?" Amber interrupts. "*Everyone* in our group is doing it. So what's up with you?"

DING DONGGGGG.

The doorbell saves Jamie from Amber's cutting remarks. "Just a sec, Amber. Someone's at the door."

Jamie sets the receiver on her nightstand and darts down the staircase. She grabs the doorknob, then takes a quick look out the peephole. She steps back and gasps.

"I can't believe it!" she mumbles to herself. "He's here! He's actually here." She takes another peek. Brad is standing on her doorstep!

She sees Brad shift his weight, glance at his watch, then press the doorbell again.

"Ah . . . c-c-coming," Jamie says. She spins around and darts halfway up the stairs, then stops. *What do I tell Amber? And how do I tell Brad he can't come in?*

DING DONG. DINGGG DONGGGGG. The doorbell rings even louder.

Good questions—and it's not just the "cool crowd" asking them anymore.

At one time or another—if you haven't already—you too will have a gut-twisting encounter like "Dustin's Dreaded Dilemma" or "Jamie's Gigantic Jam." In the face of sneers, smirks, and rolling eyes, how will *you* respond?

Pop off with a steamy, triple-X, romance-novel story and you're cool. But try explaining why you're saving your-self for the honeymoon and . . . BAM! You're suddenly treated like a MAJOR prude who's missing out on some MAJOR action. Though some guys and girls have no trouble holding their ground, for others it's worse than facing the dentist's drill.

ULTIMATE GEEK RESPONSES

- "Such earthly desires are but a thorn in my side. Yea, though I walk through the Valley of No Sex, I take up my cross and endure. It's hard to be holy, but I know that a crown awaits me in the blessed Promised Land."
- "Sex is wrong! And the minute such earthly urges pounce on my flesh, I take a cold shower. Or I deny them through Bible reading, seven-hour prayer vigils, church attendance ... and baseball."
- "Have I done *what* before? Hmmm ... er ... ahhh ... could you repeat the question? I'm just not following you. What is this 'what' you keep referring to? It? What IT? Look, we obviously aren't communicating—so I'll talk to ya later, okay? Bye now."
- "Have I had SEX?! Well ... er ... ah ... who hasn't? Hey, did ya catch that new show on the tube?"

A BETTER RESPONSE

The key is to tell the pack that you're not doing it—without being labeled "GEEK." Impossible? Not if you:

- stand confidently for what you believe—throughout your life, beginning as early as possible
- learn to present the facts and make a few key points that show why waiting is right—even smart

- cement the values you've been taught in life, and clear up any doubts swirling around inside your own head

Whether it's during a heated debate in health class, a scorching confrontation in the locker room, or a game of "phone tag" with your best friend, try this plan of action:

Don't be a geek by . . .

. . . responding with answers that begin with "The Bible sez . . ." or "Thou shalt not . . ." Not that the Bible is uncool, but as we've said, many teens don't share your belief that the Bible is the ultimate authority. Most will be instantly turned off by rules and "Bible talk." And this kind of response makes God seem like a prosecuting attorney—not a compassionate, forgiving Father.

Bottom line: communicate the truth with facts and understandable examples—not with phrases that might sound foreign to others.

. . . stepping on friends who may have blown it (and who just might be feeling a ton of guilt). Instead you should present hope and encouragement. Let your pals know that there is a better way.

. . . saying, "I don't know"—when you really do. Nothing will make you (or God) more nauseated than you being lukewarm.

GEEK-PROOF YOUR ANSWERS BY GETTING A FOOTHOLD ON THE REAL FACTS

Say something like, "I've chosen to wait, because I believe that . . .

. . . sex outside of marriage can NEVER be safe." Some guys or girls may respond, "If we use protection . . . then what's the big deal?"

Fact: condoms are not one hundred percent safe, and only reduce the risk of contracting a sexually transmitted disease (STD), such as the HIV virus that leads to AIDS. *Reducing* a risk does not mean *eliminating* it.

In the words of one doctor: "In the STD jungle, wearing a condom is safer than not wearing one, but much less safe than avoiding the jungle altogether." The truth is, beyond that thin sheath (which could break) lies disaster—even death.

. . . sex is fun, but you can't buy a condom for the heart." Many teens reduce sex to a physical act and to just another way of having fun. To them sex equals recreation. Let others know that you hold sex in high regard and don't want to cheapen this wonderful gift by giving it away to just anyone, that you're saving it for that special person who'll be your partner for life.

Fact: sex is awesome . . . in the right setting (marriage). Unlike anything else a married couple may experience, sexual intercourse creates the deepest, most powerful bond . . . sort of a relational Super Glue. And that bond is never supposed to be broken. Sex isn't just physical, and it's not a trivial act that feels good for a few seconds—and then is over for good. For a couple, sex involves the body, mind, and emotions in an activity that is intended to be shared for a lifetime.

Never buy this age-old line: "Sex will help us to really get to know each other." People who say stuff like this don't usually give a rip about the other person or about being intimate. What they really want is sex. And most girls who give in find themselves alone—until the next guy hears how far she'll go.

. . . 'sex on credit' means play now, pay later." You've probably heard one of the following comments, whether in health class or in the halls:

- "It won't hurt to do it just once."
- "Hey, diseases happen to other people."

- "I might catch something? There's probably a vaccine that'll cure it."
- "I might get pregnant? There's a place you can go to take care of it."

Fact: *today's actions* will have *consequences tomorrow.* Don't be fooled into thinking it can't happen to you; you're *not* invincible. Since the period of time it takes to die from AIDS is two to ten years, we'll probably never see *teenagers* succumb from this disease (they'll be in their twenties).

One of the most destructive and permanent results of premarital sex is acquiring a STD. And *anyone* who has sex outside of marriage (even just once) is at risk. Check out these frightening stats:

- There are more than twenty different kinds of *incurable* STDs rampant among teens.
- Experts say that of the one million to one and a half million HIV-infected Americans, more than one fifth, are teenagers.
- Sixty-three percent of all STD cases occur among persons under age twenty-five.
- In terms of being infected with STDs, if you have sex with someone who's experienced, it's like having sex with all of his or her partners.

. . . *having sex doesn't make me a man (or a woman).*" Ever see a movie or TV show in which the main characters lose their virginity . . . then go through a miraculous transformation: his voice changes, or she suddenly looks like a supermodel—and everyone treats them cool. *Yeah, right!*

Fact: you began to be a *real* man or a *real* woman at the moment of conception. Your gender is firmly a part of who you are and how you were created. Having or not having intercourse has nothing to do with it.

. . . everybody isn't doing it." But it's little wonder we get the idea everybody is. After all, Hollywood—and even our own government—bombards us with an "everybody does it" message, implying that physical intimacy goes along with dating. TV frequently shows people hopping in and out of bed, and magazines use sex to sell everything from perfume to laundry detergent.

Fact: the mass media is feeding us a lie—and many of our friends are buying into it. But often the steamy stories that guys tell in the locker room are just that—stories. If you're saving sex for the wedding night, you're not alone. Many other teens on your campus have chosen not to be sexually active.

. . . I'm not weird if I wait." And you won't get sick, go crazy, or die if you don't have sex. Remember, sex is a drive, not a need. You need air and food to survive, but you can live a full and happy life without sex. Be assured that all the essential parts work—you don't need a test run.

Fact: unlike dogs, cats, and other members of the animal kingdom, who are slaves to their instincts (and who seem to go berserk during mating season), humans are given free choice *and* self-control. God expects us—and helps us—to control our desires and wait for his timing and his best plans for us.

The Lord hasn't given us meaningless guidelines in order to make life boring. And his rules are never dusty or out-of-date. His timeless instructions are intended to protect us from harm and to insure that we get the most out of the gifts that he provides—such as sex. He's our number one fan and wants us to be happy.

You won't be disappointed—or a geek—if you wait. We guarantee it!

ON YOUR OWN

1. Crack open your Bible and check out Leviticus 18:3, 6, 20, 22–24.

   ✎ Name some sexual practices that are off-limits to believers.

   ✎ From these passages, why do you think God wants Christians to stay pure in such an impure world?

2. Read 1 Corinthians 5:1–13. What will happen to those who don't follow God's guidelines—especially regarding sex?

3. Take a look at 1 Thessalonians 4:3–5 and Ephesians 5:3. Name some sexual standards that God expects of those who wear the label "Christian."

4. Read Romans 7:15. Exactly what is the battle that Paul is talking about?

5. Turn to Zechariah 4:6. This Scripture passage reminds us that it is not by our might or by our power but by the Holy Spirit that we are able to withstand temptation. Yes, we'll all fail from time to time. *But when we allow the power of God to help us, we can stand firm.*

Write a prayer to God, asking him to give you strength to stand firm in your faith, and power to resist sexual temptation.

WITH A GROUP

1. What is God's real view on sex?

2. Have different members of your group read the following passages: Leviticus 19:29, Proverbs

6:25–29, 32–33, and Deuteronomy 23:17–18. Next tackle these questions:

- ✎ How does God describe prostitution?
- ✎ Why is adultery off-limits for Christians?
- ✎ In what ways is sex outside of marriage destructive?

3. Take turns reading portions of Genesis 39 until finished. Now answer these questions:

- ✎ What lessons can we learn from Joseph?
- ✎ In what ways is Joseph a good role model?
- ✎ Will you always be congratulated for taking a stand?

4. Name ten differences between love and lust. (See 1 Corinthians 13:4–7 for some clues.)

5. How far is too far? (Check out 1 Thessalonians 4:3–7 for some ideas.)

8

Put a Sock in It

Lunches and dinners in my (Greg's) college dorms resembled some kind of sick game show. Every day, the guys would gather around two tables in the dining room at the very end of the hall. While they ate, they kept their eyes focused down a long corridor that led from the chow line to the various dining rooms for the other dorms. As soon as a girl came down the hallway, carrying her tray, the rating game would heat up.

"Back to your macaroni and cheese, guys. She's only a four."

"No way. She's at least a seven."

"What are you guys, the blind brothers? She gets a two. But check out the babe coming down now. She's a definite nine."

"Who's that girl with her?"

"It's her roommate. There must be a rule when they divide up students: a gorgeous girl has to room with a dog."

"Except sometimes they make mistakes. See these next two girls. They're roommates. Look at them. What do you think they need most, a paper bag over their heads or a leash?"

All the guys would then bust up laughing.

Every day was like that! Whoever could come up with the crudest remarks about the girls walking down the hallway was king. If you gave a girl a low number, you had to justify it with some comment about her ancestry. Most of the girls probably never knew what was going on (but a lot were smart enough to stay clear of our dorm cafeteria).

Had it been a year earlier, I probably would have joined in. But I became a Christian during my freshman year, and I just didn't feel right about this game. In fact, it really bugged me. Girls were being analyzed as if they were objects or animals. I knew most of these guys, and they didn't just talk that way, they treated girls the same way. They used them (or wanted to), and showed no more respect for them than a criminal does for a victim. Was it harmless male "fun" or a habit too ingrained to break? Actually, neither.

GUYS AREN'T ALONE

Though I've never actually been to one, I've heard enough stories about what happens at girls' slumber parties to know that crude college guys aren't the only ones with a rating system. (Some girls are kinder, of course . . . as are many guys.) For girls there's not the same macho pressure to belittle someone. But if a girl wants to get a laugh . . .

"I would absolutely die if Jeff Crane called and asked me to the game."

"You and a hundred others, girl. Forget about his booty, because he doesn't even know that you exist."

"Or the rest of us, for that matter!"

"Yeah, but what about Steve Parsons? Now there's a guy we'd all have a chance to date—and he's cute, too."

"Except for you, Sally, right? Don't you think a boy like Jerome Needlemeir would be *your* dream date?"

"Needlemeir! He's a freshman, and he's got glasses! I think Steve Urkel look-alikes are more your speed, Angie!"

Well, I guess you had to be there. But you get the point, don't you? Girls can sometimes be just as cruel as guys when it comes to the rating game.

ULTIMATE GEEK RESPONSES

Are Christians immune from joining in on comparing one person's "earthsuit" with another's?

Immune, no. Tempted, yes. Do they join in? Sometimes.

I could give a dozen more examples of what is said by one sex about the other, but you likely hear it every day in the hallways. If you don't hear it, you see it. That's right, see it. The girls who have a pretty face or are "well developed," skinnier, or "okay-looking but outgoing" are nearly always given a second look (stare!) by guys.

In the same way, guys who are athletes, who have nice clothes or a hot car, who don't wear nerdy-looking glasses, who have a buff bod—these guys are the ones who turn the heads of the popular females.

Let's admit it: in twentieth-century North America, this is a game that will *always* be played. It's too deep within our culture for us not to gaze on "better-looking" outward appearances and be attracted by them. It's not fair. I don't like it. God doesn't like it. But it ain't going to change.

Therefore I think that all Christian teens—to show that they're *really* Christians—should start talking to and dating plain or "ugly" classmates. Okay? You'll do that for me, won't you?

NO? Well, what if I promise that God will reward you richly if you do?

What? Still no?

Now back to reality

I realize it's too much to ask of you to start paying more attention—or consider becoming friends with—those of the opposite sex whom your peer group would normally never even talk to. I could perhaps make you feel guilty by saying, "What would Jesus do?" But that would likely only make you put the book down and think, *This guy is NOT living in reality!*

SO WHAT IS REALITY?

Christians, who believe that God created each individual for a unique purpose, look like total geeks when they play the verbal and nonverbal rating game.

It's impossible to never make a mistake. But for the most part, our words and actions should represent God accurately—especially when it comes to treating people the way Jesus would. We're the only picture that people have when they want to know what God looks like. They won't go to church, they definitely DON'T watch Christian TV, and they often won't read the letters of the Bible. But what they WILL read is you. The apostle Paul said, *"You yourselves are our letter, written on our hearts, known and read by everybody. You show that you are a letter from Christ, the result of our ministry, written not with ink but with the Spirit of the living God, not on tablets of stone but on tablets of human hearts"* (2 Corinthians 3:2–3).

Most people will realize that even Christians aren't perfect (good thing!), but even though people may be experts themselves at verbal abuse, they are a little less tolerant of Christians who make deliberate choices to devalue others.

Showing respect is the issue. Yes, I know that in your group, it may not be too cool to hold your tongue—or keep your eyes focused straight ahead—but you must make the effort if you don't want to be a Christian geek.

THE RESPECT THANG

So far, this chapter has hit on respect issues between guys and girls. So what are some ways to show the opposite sex—or people in general—the respect they deserve as special creations of God? Start here:

Stay quiet about body parts. The first guy to notice and say something about the size of specific parts of the female anatomy usually gets the laugh. Let's be honest: do we really need to say anything about parts a girl has no control over? Is it really worth it to comment on something that everyone already knows? How intelligent will you actually look?

This is a tough area for guys, no doubt. Keeping yourself from thinking these thoughts is even tougher. But when you say something, it reveals what's in your heart. If you have to make a comment every time you see something you like or don't like about the body parts of girls, then it will be obvious to all: you've got sex on the brain.

Yes, it's normal—and okay—to be attracted to a pretty face or a nice body, but it shows a big-time character flaw to be talking about it all the time. Once you've dug yourself into the habit of always having to comment, you begin to look at girls as objects to be used, instead of as REAL PEOPLE who deserve respect. Frankly, it's a habit that's tough to break once it gets started. If a guy is serious about representing his faith to his friends, one clear way to show a difference is to keep quiet about such things.

This type of humor is coming more and more from the mouths of girls. As TV, movies, and music become more explicit, it's tough not to join in. Don't be a geek. Fight the urge, ladies!

Realize that half-joking remarks aren't really harmless. This proverb says it best: "Like a madman shooting firebrands or deadly arrows is a man who deceives his neighbor and says, 'I was only joking!'" (Proverbs 26:18–19).

Things said half-jokingly in the presence of friends or strangers aren't as harmless as we think. Words hurt, especially if you're on the receiving end. A smile or saying, "Hey, I was just kiddin'" doesn't always ease the pain, either.

This type of humor, called sarcasm, is practically a way of life for some. Is all of it bad? No, it's not. If we direct it toward ourselves in a fun way, toward a ridiculous commercial or TV show, or toward a person who is so emotionally close to us that there is no way they could take it as a cutting remark, then it can be okay. But all too often it's simply a way of saying something negative without appearing to be mean. Sarcastic cuts are basically putdowns—and they can be very mean.

The best way to know if your sarcasm isn't cool is to ask a good friend if what you're saying hurts . . . or if it's no big deal. "Hey, you know how I'm sarcastic a lot with you and the other guys. Does it bug you? How about them? Well, if I ever go overboard, let me know, okay?"

Having a friend whom you've given permission to keep you accountable in this area is a good idea.

Whenever possible, put in a good word for the underdog. The kids in school that are sometimes treated like verbal punching bags need a defender. Not only should you NOT join in, perhaps you could stick up for them. Defending the defenseless is courageous work, and not every Christian teen has what it takes to speak up. How about you? What would be the worst possible consequence if you were to tell the verbal boxers at school to put a sock in it?

How should you do it?

Probably not while the *group* is still throwing insults. Find a few minutes alone with the worst offenders (it's usually a few who cause others to join in). Let them know that it makes you uncomfortable, that it's not right to rip on others—and ask them if they could put a lid on it. Tell them that their words are cutting this person deeply. Try to bring them around to your way of thinking. Hopefully, they'll go along.

If the group is getting out of hand, you may have to take immediate action. To jump in and change the subject so that you get everyone's mind focused on something else is a good first step. If that doesn't work, you may have to take a BIG risk: *"You guys are acting like jerks. What did this guy ever do to deserve this type of abuse? All you're doing is putting someone else down to make yourselves look good. It's weak. It's lame. I expect better things out of my friends, so knock it off."*

> "Cold words freeze people, and hot words scorch them, and bitter words make them bitter, and wrathful words make them wrathful. Kind words also produce their own image on men's souls; and a beautiful image it is. They soothe, quiet and comfort the hearer."
>
> BLAISE PASCAL

Whoa! Saying that *is* pretty risky. What if they turn their tongues on you? Well, isn't standing up for what's right—and defending someone Jesus died for—sometimes worth that big a risk? If your friends dump you, they will have probably done you a favor. Remember: "Bad company corrupts good character" (1 Corinthians 15:33).

When others are ranking on adult authority figures, don't join in. You've probably heard someone call a police officer a pig. Principals, vice-principals, teachers, coaches, and some other kid's parents are easy targets of verbal abuse. It's true that *some* adults aren't always too nice, and they sometimes won't treat you the way you would treat them, but fight the urge to put them down. Here's a passage that explains why it's the best idea to respect those in authority over you:

Everyone must submit himself to the governing authorities, for there is no authority except that which God has established.

The authorities that exist have been established by God. Consequently, he who rebels against the authority is rebelling against what God has instituted, and those who do so will bring judgment on themselves. For rulers hold no terror for those who do right, but for those who do wrong. Do you want to be free from fear of the one in authority? Then do what is right and he will commend you.

ROMANS 13:1–3

Be the friend that everyone would like to have. What type of people do you like to be around? Someone who's negative all the time, who always finds something wrong with others, and who never encourages anyone? Or someone who's positive and optimistic, who looks for the good in others, and who makes a habit of being an encourager?

No, you don't have to get syrupy all the time or be so sickly sweet in your personality that you drip honey, but being "UP" will likely win you more friends than you know what to do with.

If you like hangin' with friends who give you a positive word once in a while . . . start handing out positive stuff! Point out the good things you see in others. Don't talk about anyone behind their back. Smile a little more. Be good-natured in your joking instead of cruel. And above all, try not to join your friends in rating members of the opposite sex.

ON YOUR OWN

1. Name those people in your life whose opinion about you really counts.

2. Write down what you think God's opinion is of you.

3. What are God's feelings for your friends—girls and guys—at school?

4. How do you think God feels when he sees his creations put down, or viewed as sex objects?

5. Read 1 John 4:20 and Proverbs 11:9. Name three ways these two passages come true at school.

✎

✎

✎

WITH A GROUP

1. Each one answer the five questions in the "On Your Own" section. When you're done, discuss what you wrote. Then name as many ways as you can think of how Christian guys and girls can show respect for one another.

2. Will God hold us accountable for our words? (See Matthew 12:36–37.)

3. How can Christians help each other keep that level of respect high and treat others the way they were designed to be treated? (Look up James 3:1–12 and see if you can spot five principles.)

4. In what situations are people most tempted to say things that devalue others?

5. If a person makes a commitment to start showing some verbal respect for friends, strangers, adults, et cetera, what do you think the rewards will be? The consequences?

9

Altering the Life That God Intended

A DIRECT ASSAULT

Here's an actual letter that a *Breakaway* reader wrote to us not long ago:

Dear Breakaway,

I go to a school near a military base. For the past few weeks, we've been discussing discrimination in my English class. One of the projects we had to do was a debate. Our teacher gave us the choice of topics and the chance to be either positive or negative. The topic I chose was "Should homosexuals be allowed in the armed forces?" I took the negative side.

In my school, I've been known to stand up for my faith. After the debate, we had to write an argumentative essay on the topic we chose. In mine, I included three things: what most people believe, what soldiers think, and what the Bible says. After handing in the essay I had worked hard on, I was stunned when the teacher gave me a C+. The comment she wrote was shocking. It said I started off well but ended it poorly when I talked about the Bible's law against homosexuals.

When I went to complain to the teacher, she explained, "I'm a Christian like you, and I've read in the Bible that masters should be kind to their slaves. Today we don't have slaves; therefore the Bible is wrong. That means that homosexuality should be allowed today. If Christ came down, he would probably change the law on homosexuals. Paul was a homosexual and preached that the Bible may be wrong."

I told her that the Bible never said you must or must not own a slave, yet it does say that homosexuality is a sin. She told me that was silly. I couldn't imagine a teacher would say another student's beliefs were silly.

I've already left this event behind, and I'm not trying to get back at her. However, I would like to know what your opinion is, and get a better understanding on what the Bible really thinks about homosexuals. In my debate, I expressed that Satan was controlling their lives. Was that a good idea?

ULTIMATE GEEK RESPONSES

- "All this talk about alternative lifestyles, and guys wanting to have sex with guys, is making me sick! These are people who have an obvious mental problem. They're in serious need of counseling."
- "My pastor says that homosexuals are an abomination to God. He thinks that God is going to judge our entire nation because we're not only tolerating these people, our own government is

calling evil good and good evil. He thinks that
unless we start speaking out against these people,
we're all going to pay."

- "If you ask me, we ought to send them all to San
Francisco and let earthquakes or AIDS take care
of them. Or a better idea would be to line them all
up and shoot 'em, like Hitler did."

A BETTER IDEA

Everyone notices if you launch an ignorant statement
like the ones above—since they carry the attitude that
you're judging someone else (and everyone knows that
you're not perfect).

Whether a discussion on this issue occurs in class or
with a group of friends, the best approach is to ask questions
that might put doubts in the mind of someone who hasn't
thought through the issue. The "undecideds" are types who
are often willing to accept what the group has to say.

Depending on where you are when a discussion
breaks out, here are a few questions you can try:

- "If homosexuality is normal for some and not for
others, and since you don't believe there is
anything unique about the human race as a
creation [assuming you know this about the
person], then why are there only a couple of
examples in the *entire* animal world of same-sex
unions?"
- "Could one conclude that homosexuality is a
learned behavior—based on a person's
background, upbringing, or thought-life—versus
an inbred one? Haven't those studies on the
inbred theory been challenged by mainstream
scientists because the studies were thought to be
biased?"

- "What other nations have viewed a sexual minority as a protected class, the way African-Americans, Hispanics, or Asians are viewed in the U.S.? Do pedophiles receive the same protection?"
- "If God created homosexuals, why didn't he openly recognize them in the Bible? 'In the beginning . . .' could have been written differently. Why, then, does he uphold marriage as the way for society?"
- "Most homosexual men have hundreds of partners in their lifetime, especially when they're younger. Doesn't their behavior show they're not interested in forming a committed relationship but only interested in pursuing pleasure?"

What does the Bible say about homosexuals?

There are a few passages that mention homosexuality directly:

Do you not know that the wicked will not inherit the kingdom of God? Do not be deceived: Neither the sexually immoral nor idolaters nor adulterers nor male prostitutes nor homosexual offenders nor thieves nor the greedy nor drunkards nor slanderers nor swindlers will inherit the kingdom of God. And that is what some of you were. But you were washed, you were sanctified, you were justified in the name of the Lord Jesus Christ and by the Spirit of our God.

1 CORINTHIANS 6:9–11

As you can see, homosexuality has been occurring for a long time. Whatever wonderful gifts God has created (like sex between a husband and a wife), humans have been known to corrupt. In this passage, homosexuality is lumped together with several other behaviors that God finds detestable. These are things that members of the Corinthian church *used* to practice. But Paul makes the point that they are all forgivable deeds, doesn't he?

Paul is equally clear on what the consequences are for those who continue to practice such things. (FYI: It's unlikely that Paul would announce the consequences of his own behavior if he were homosexual. Though he did choose to remain single in order to have more freedom to spread the gospel, he was in no way a homosexual.)

The next passage—also written by Paul—is even clearer:

They exchanged the truth of God for a lie, and worshiped and served created things rather than the Creator—who is forever praised. Amen.

Because of this, God gave them over to shameful lusts. Even their women exchanged natural relations for unnatural ones. In the same way the men also abandoned natural relations with women and were inflamed with lust for one another. Men committed indecent acts with other men, and received in themselves the due penalty for their perversion. . . .

Although they know God's righteous decree that those who do such things deserve death, they not only continue to do these very things but also approve of those who practice them.

ROMANS 1:25–27, 32

Having relations with someone of the same sex is not just indecent, it's unnatural. God's truth is that he created us male and female for a reason: to populate the earth, to keep us from becoming lonely, and to enable us to enjoy each other's unique differences.

If someone persists in following their own lusts instead of God's ideal, they are allowed to "reap what they've sown." God won't control a person's choices, no matter if those choices lead to a destructive conclusion. Why? He loves his creations too much to keep us as puppets. He wants us to choose to follow and obey him, not out of fear but out of love for all that he has done.

Should you question a teacher who gives you a bad grade based on his or her personal opinions on moral issues?

Yes, as long as it's done respectfully. This person did the right thing by going to the teacher in private and inquiring about her comments. In reality, her comments were totally out of line and subjective—at best. But . . . she's the teacher. Unless the student decided to press the issue of the C+ and go over her head, there wasn't much more to be done.

Is Satan controlling the lives of homosexuals—and is that a good argument to use?

There's a fine line between "control" and "influence." One passage says this: "We know that we are children of God, and that the whole world is under the control of the evil one" (1 John 5:19). This is the only Bible verse that talks about what Satan has control of. It sounds like he does control those who are still living according to this world, and 2 Corinthians 4:4 backs that up: "The god of this age has blinded the minds of unbelievers, so that they cannot see the light of the gospel of the glory of Christ, who is the image of God."

In another passage, Paul says this about people who were then Christians but used to be idol worshipers: "You know that when you were pagans, somehow or other you were influenced and led astray to mute idols" (1 Corinthians 12:2). Yet it doesn't say they were controlled, does it?

Since God doesn't control a person's will, we don't believe Satan has that power, either. However, if someone is not seeking God's light, they are susceptible to Satan's blinding influence. He plants lies in their mind, lies that turn into thoughts, attitudes, and eventually actions. He knows that taking someone deeper into a sinful, dark lifestyle is like taking them to the bottom of the sea. If you're twenty or thirty feet deep, you can still look up and see a vague light toward the surface. But if you're two hundred feet deep, you can see no light at all.

Some Christians understand this satanic strategy, but non-Christians don't. The reason: they're underwater, seeing spiritual things in a blurred fog. It's true that most unbelievers aren't down as deep as someone involved in homosexuality, but they're far from the light of God's love and truth. For this reason, Satan's influence is not a good argument to use around them.

What can you say when someone has come to the wrong conclusion about Christians and how they treat practicing homosexuals?

In many parts of the country, this issue is front-page news on a weekly basis. Naturally, the liberal media portray Christians as narrow-minded hate-mongers. Our worldview is that the homosexual lifestyle isn't what God intended for us (and is a deadly choice). Christians are ridiculed and accused of not being as "enlightened" as Hollywood elite.

To be honest, some Christians *have* acted like geeks around unbelievers on this issue. They've said things in the wrong way or have even made hurtful statements about homosexuals to the media. That's the main reason that Christians have acquired this bad reputation. Even when we're attempting to be rational and kind, we're often lumped into this mold whether we like it or not.

Christians are in a BIG dilemma.

On the one hand, we should love, forgive, and try to help those who are caught in this deadly lifestyle. We also need to remember that we have sins of our own; and for this reason, we are commanded not to judge other human beings made in the image of God.

On the other hand, not only are open, practicing homosexuals tougher to reach out to, there is within the movement a growing militancy that is fed up with what they perceive as discrimination. They want the exact same rights as heterosexuals, and they'll stoop to any tactic to attain them. Organizations like ACT-UP, Queer Nation, and Lesbian Avengers have been known to use intimidation and violence to make Christians (as well as the undecided) fearful of expressing their convictions.

What "rights" do they want? They want to be able to adopt children. Whether they're married or just living together, they want the same governmental privileges as any couple would receive. They want books in school libraries to portray the homosexual lifestyle as healthy and normal. Mostly they want to be looked at as a minority and thus as eligible for special rights like African-Americans or the handicapped have.

The problem with the homosexual and lesbian desire for minority status is that they're a minority based on their sexual *preference*. If local, state, or federal governments begin to give them protected status, then they will have to give minority status to other groups: smokers, drinkers, cross-country skiers, Baptists, Catholics, et cetera. The point is obvious: no one should be protected by the government on the basis of a lifestyle choice. Yet this is the radical homosexual agenda that will be arriving in nearly every town and city in the country within the next five years. It is extremely well-funded and organized (more so than the Christian agenda).

What should the Christian response to this *radical agenda* be?

If we don't speak up about this powerful group, our schools and cities will crumble. If homosexuals are called a protected and abused minority, then job quotas will follow. That means that businesses (even Christian-owned businesses) will be forced to hire homosexuals in numbers proportionate to the percentage of homosexuals in the population.

The radical homosexual groups are also lobbying school boards to allow them to enter the classroom and present their case there. They want to counsel teenagers who have considered this question: "I've had *thoughts* about what it would be like to get sexual with my same sex. Does that mean I'm a homosexual?"

The answer these groups would like to present is, "Yes . . . and that's okay. You were born that way; don't fight it." This is recruiting, plain and simple.

What about the argument that homosexuals and lesbians are born that way, that it's not just a choice? Hasn't science proved this to be true?

We have received a couple of letters in which the person writing says they have "gay feelings." That is, for a very brief time as they awaken sexually, they are more attracted to the same sex than to the opposite sex. This is common for a very small percentage of teens. If this attraction is combined with emotional or environmental factors, then a teen may continue to lean toward homosexuality.

In research for this book, we spoke with an ex-homosexual. He told us that's what happened to him. He felt an attraction to males, but he also said that there were other problems that pushed him in that direction. Pornography played a huge role in making him attracted to other guys. His father could not show appropriate affection for him (having been molested in childhood, and because his own father didn't know how to show him affection). At age twelve he was exposed to homosexual videos—then molested—by a neighbor. All along the way, he had no one with whom to talk these feelings through. He was alone.

At age twenty-one he went into the homosexual lifestyle and found that nearly every other homosexual or lesbian he met had similar influences. (The women, he said, often had been molested by a man that they had trusted. Plus they'd had difficulty forming good relationships with boys their own age.)

He said that it all started with wrong thought-patterns that could not be discussed. Combined with the other factors, this pushed him over the edge.

Regarding the well-publicized argument that homosexuals are born and not made, here are the facts: Every bit of research that the press has reported on has been done *by* a homosexual, *for* homosexuals. Many studies have been done by homosexuals dying of AIDS and wanting to prove something before they go. There simply haven't been enough credible studies done over a long enough period of time and by unbiased researchers to point to any conclusions.

So how exactly should Christian students respond when they are hit with this issue?

Since the radical end of the homosexual movement does not have widespread acceptance in the public schools like it does in much of the media, what Christian students will likely be confronted with is this:

1. Classroom discussions in which a teacher or a few students take up "the cause."

2. A confused—and often silent—classmate who is either "in the closet" (hiding their homosexual practices, which is more common) or open about their sexual choices.

Christians who have thought through their response, have consulted what the Bible says about loving sinners, and aren't trying to put others down in order to make themselves look good will usually take the high road. That is, they'll preface every comment or argument with something like this:

> We're all human, and everyone makes choices
> that aren't always healthy for them. I've learned that

God is very forgiving when we're able to admit that what we've done is wrong. But I can't in good conscience agree that these choices are God's best. Isn't it true that none of us would agree that the choice of sharing needles to use illegal drugs is the right choice? The virus that causes AIDS is epidemic among those who do this. So why would I say that practicing homosexuality is any better? What I'd really be saying is, "Fine, let them do what they want, they're all going to die a horrible death anyway. They deserve what they get."

I may not always act like it, but I say I care for people because Jesus Christ died for them; so why would I approve of this choice that causes so many young people—that God created—to die a slow, agonizing death?

This can be an emotional issue. But logic can prevail— even for Christians. The logic of compassion, forgiveness, and kindness will always be the correct response on moral issues such as this.

In biblical days, Jesus touched those with leprosy, spent time with the vilest of sinners, and condemned people only if they were hypocrites. If he were here today, he'd aggressively confront the wrong he witnessed (the money changers at the temple, for example), but he'd be equally aggressive in loving those trapped in sin (the woman caught in adultery in John 8).

Our advice is to go light on confrontation and heavy on love.

ON YOUR OWN

1. Look up these passages and paraphrase what they say:

   ✎ Leviticus 18:22

   ✎ Deuteronomy 23:18

   ✎ Ephesians 5:5–6

2. Based on the passages you have read so far in this chapter, is homosexuality a worse sin than any other, in the eyes of God? Why? Why not?

3. Look up the following three passages. Answer yes if they apply to those who are practicing the homosexual lifestyle, no if they don't.

   ✎ John 3:16   Yes_____   No_____

   ✎ John 10:9–11   Yes_____   No_____

   ✎ Luke 23:34   Yes_____   No_____

4. Based on these passages, as well as others you have read, what does God think of those who are trapped in this behavior?

5. What do you think holds Christians back from treating or accepting the homosexual the way Jesus Christ would?

WITH A GROUP

Look up the passages and discuss the questions in the "On Your Own" section.

1. Three of the four Scriptures mentioned in the first question above come from the Old Testament. Do passages like this apply to life in your world? Why? Why not?

2. What attitudes displayed by Christians have you observed, regarding homosexuals?

3. How can Christians learn to deal with their fears and prejudices on this issue?

4. What do you think is the ideal response that Christians should have toward homosexuals?

5. How about our response toward those in school who think that the only thing all Christians do is judge and condemn? What should we say? What would be the best attitude to have?

10

Exposing New Age Nonsense

Snapshot #1: Two girls in first-period English have their eyes glued to the horoscope section of a popular teen magazine. They start asking for everyone's birthday so they can tell them their horoscope.

Snapshot #2: A clerk at the mall bookstore posts a flyer advertising a "human potential" workshop.

Snapshot #3: In health class, the school nurse launches into the same old lecture about "holistic health" and how you really should look into it.

Snapshot #4: Your best friend catches her mom sitting on the living room floor chanting, "I am god. I am god."

Are any of these "snapshots" somewhere in your "memory album"? If you just nodded yes, then you've had a modern-day encounter with an age-old error: New Age.

Check out the following strange scenario. (Hey, it's not from the files of the Twilight Zone. It's actually happening to guys and girls like YOU all across the country!)

ORBITING THE OZONE

Chris hustles into her art class and takes a seat with the other students at the worktable—just as usual. But as she pulls her sketchpad out of her backpack and glances up at the teacher, that's when it hits her: things aren't usual at all. *This is strange*, she thinks. *Verrry STRANGE!*

The instructor is sitting in a chair facing the class. His eyes are squeezed shut and his head is tilted back. His arms and legs are crossed at the wrists and ankles, yoga-style. He slowly exhales, then takes long, deep breaths (just like a weight lifter concentrating on repetitions).

The skeptical students exchange stunned smirks and puzzled looks. Others let out sarcastic remarks.

"Is he having, like . . . a diabetic seizure or something?" someone whispers.

"More like brain meltdown," fires back another voice.

Uh-oh, what's Mr. Sullivan up to? Chris wonders. *He sometimes seems like his head is somewhere in the ozone layer, but this time—YIKES!*

And the words scribbled on the chalkboard are even more bizarre:

Meditation is man's search for understanding of the
    universe and
his own place within it. This has led man to explore
    the internal world:
the realm of his mind. Meditation can provide self-
    awareness, leading to
inner peace and a sense of unity with creation.

"Okay, my future artists," the teacher says, breaking out of his trancelike state and hopping to his feet. "To those of you who thought I just lost my mind—WRONG! I focused it . . . achieving unity and peace with creation. Now I'm ready to tackle the task at hand—artistic expression."

Chris shifts her weight and nervously taps her pencil on her sketchpad. *Somethin's seriously wrong here, Lord.*

"You see, meditation is like this tool," Mr. Sullivan says, holding up a sable-hair paintbrush. He then points to his description on the chalkboard. "It enables me to unlock my true potential within. Everyone has awesome potential inside. Even you."

The teacher looks right at Chris. "We reach it only when we empty the negative thoughts swirling around upstairs. Then we can visualize the masterpieces we're going to paint."

Mr. Sullivan pops a tape into his boom box. "Before we go to work this period, I want you to give meditation a try. This will tell you how to get started."

Chris slouches in her chair and slides her sunglasses on. *Help, Lord! I can't let this stuff invade my mind. I've got to speak up. But how? And will the teacher—or anyone else—even listen?*

ULTIMATE GEEK RESPONSES

- "Sorry, Teacher, but you've obviously been dipping more than just your brush in the turpentine. It's time to get out of the ozone, pal!"
- "Meditate on this, friends: Satan is leading you straight to hell. You're being deceived—BIG TIME!"
- "Is the school board aware of what you're up to? Perhaps I should educate them about your Twilight Zone techniques."

A BETTER RESPONSE

Despite its name, the so-called New Age movement is actually selling an incredibly ancient lie. Much of its philosophy is based on Hindu beliefs that existed long before Jesus came to save the world.

Those who buy the New Age lie will often swallow hair-raising ideas, like "Everybody is a god" or "Look inward for power and healing." But what's even scarier is that this dangerous invasion from the East is gaining thousands of converts in the West. It's also infiltrating nearly every sector of society: medicine, science, business, entertainment . . . even the classroom.

Even if Chris' brush with the bizarre seems a bit extreme—and even if the New Age movement isn't noticeable at your school—sooner or later you'll come into contact with it. And like it or not, it has found its way into the chalkboard jungle. We want to arm you with the truth so you can steer clear of the nonsense.

So what's the best approach?

Understand that your teacher isn't the deceiver. He's the deceived. He's probably doing his best to improve the educational climate in his class. He may not be religious at all but has latched onto this because it sounds good. Pray for him and be willing to ask why he's doing what he does.

If you are asked to close your eyes and concentrate, pray instead and concentrate on God's Word. In your mind, recite all the verses you know. Then ask God to change the atmosphere in your classroom. Put on the armor of God and be firm in your prayers.

The Bible is the key to defeating the enemy. Satan knows this and will try any tactic to keep you from having a quiet time with Jesus. Study Ephesians 6:10–18. It describes the tools you need to stand firm. In fact, memorize it by learning one verse a week, so your "sword" will be ready at all times.

Find support from Christian teachers, your parents, your pastor, or your youth leader. Tell them what's going on in your class. The adults in your church are just as concerned as you are about New Age practices infiltrating your school.

Talk to your teacher. Respectfully point out the Eastern roots of some of the things he is asking you to do. Suggest that if other religious practices—such as Bible reading and prayer—are outlawed in school, this should be, too. If necessary, join with other Christian students and ask to be excused from visualizing and meditating.

Be aware. Learn what the New Age is and isn't. That's the goal of the rest of this chapter.

SO EXACTLY HOW CAN ALL THIS NEW AGE STUFF HURT?

After all, some of it sounds pretty cool . . . even in tune with Christianity. Check out these common New Age goals:

- Achieve peace, harmony, and brotherhood in a world marked by turmoil and strife.
- Get in tune with "God" and become all "he" designed you to be.
- Clear away "bad thoughts, negative emotions, and anything else that fogs up your mind," by focusing your energy on what is "good, pure, and lovely."

New Age philosophies often use Christian lingo, biblical ideas and teachings, and even parts of the Bible itself. And most New Agers don't deny the existence of Jesus Christ or that he is God's Son. On top of that, New Age ideas appeal to a hunger for spiritual experience and to the yearning for a better tomorrow. These are valid desires and worthy goals. But there's one gigantic problem for Christians: **this whole movement rejects the real God of the Bible.**

According to the New Age, truth is found not by reading God's Word but by looking within yourself. Whatever truth you find by looking within—New Agers claim—is the right truth for you.

Once you sort through all the positive-thinking techniques, ozone phrases, and Christian-sounding concepts, you eventually discover something dark and empty. Christian author Bill Myers puts it this way: "You discover that New Age thinking can be boiled down to one thing: it's simply a hodgepodge of demonic practices from the Eastern religions, with just enough Christianity thrown in so we'll swallow the bait. Unfortunately, it isn't until the bait goes down that people discover there's a hook buried inside."

WARNING SIGNS

The following statements should serve as warning signals. The minute someone coughs out phrases like these—whether at school or at that healthy salad shop just off campus (you know, the place where you can actually eat and not have a major zit attack)—your head should explode with sirens, flare guns, bells, whistles, fireworks . . . ANYTHING that triggers this message: "WARNING: ALL BRAIN CELLS REPORT TO BATTLE STATIONS. DANGEROUS PHILOSOPHIES ABOUT TO ENTER CEREBRAL SECTOR."

"We are one with Mother Earth." According to New Agers, there's no separation between humanity and nature or between humans and God.

"God is an impersonal energy or force." That was the ongoing theme of *Star Wars*, the blockbuster movie of the seventies. Here are some other terms that are often

thrown around: Life Force, Higher Consciousness, Higher Self, the Self, Mind at Large, Supermind, Universal Mind.

"We are all 'God' whether we recognize it or not." Many popular actors in Hollywood have bought this lie.

"Jesus was just a good teacher." Most New Agers link Jesus Christ with religious figures like Buddha and Mohammed. It's not uncommon to hear statements like, "Jesus, like many other great masters, was an ordinary man who became a master of wisdom."

"A consciousness revolution achieved through meditation unlocks the divine within." Popular programs include e.s.t., rebirthing, Silva mind control, human potential workshops, chanting, and various massage therapies. These techniques are often offshoots of Eastern religions, such as Buddhism, Hinduism, and Taoism.

TUNING IN TO THE RIGHT SOURCE

Popular speaker Josh McDowell says this about the New Age movement: "It is evidence that men and women are still making the same mistake since the Garden of Eden. The Genesis account relates how Satan, in the guise of a serpent, promised Adam and Eve that if they ate the forbidden fruit, they would 'be like God, knowing good and evil.' But Satan, the inventor of the half-truth, lied. They did not become like God."

God's Word—the Bible—slam-dunks New Age nonsense, with the news that Jesus, "being in very nature God, did not consider equality with God something to be grasped, but made himself nothing. . . . And being found in appearance as a man, he humbled himself and became obedient to death—even death on a cross!" (Philippians 2:6–8).

In other words, the rock-solid, time-tested message of the Bible is not that people can become gods but that God became a man and died for our sins so that we can have eternal life—the ultimate good news.

NEW AGE BASICS

Now that you have a grasp on why the New Age is off-base and know the warning signals, let's arm you with the facts. Here are a few New Age basics you should be aware of:

Channeling and talking with the dead

What it's all about. Some people claim that ancient seers (or wise men) communicate with them, using their mind and body. You've probably heard about these individuals on TV talk shows.

For example, a woman in Washington state claims that a thirty-five-thousand-year-old "spiritual" teacher named Ramtha speaks through her. Some folks pay hundreds of dollars to see performances by channelers like her. ("Channeler" is another term for what the Bible calls a "medium.")

Why it's the WRONG channel. This whole practice involves one thing: demon possession. Those who channel are NOT dealing with friendly little "Yodas" or E.T.-type critters who want to help them have an awesome life. These spirits are evil and use any kind of deception and dirty trick they can to gain control of a person's mind, body, and soul. A demon's goal is to separate men and women from God and to send them on a fast track straight to—you guessed it—eternal darkness (hell).

Demonic spirits always take more than they give. So tell your friends not to fool around with this stuff. Because once they invite a demon to lunch, there's a good chance it won't be leaving.

What the Bible says. "Let no one be found among you who sacrifices his son or daughter in the fire, who practices divination or sorcery, interprets omens, engages in witchraft, or casts spells, or who is a medium or spiritist or who consults the dead. Anyone who does these things is detestable to the LORD" (Deuteronomy 18:10–12a).

Reincarnation

What it's all about. People who buy this lie think that after death, each person returns to an endless series of lives as different people. So if you were a good person in the past life, things are going to go better for you this time around. If you were a jerk the last time, you'll pay for it by having to come back as a bottom-of-the-heap person. Most New Agers want very much to believe this. They think it will give them another chance to live a better life or to make up for a sin they've committed.

Why it's a dead-end belief. Reincarnation is in direct opposition to the Bible. God makes it clear that we live just ONE life in our earthsuits, die, and are then judged by God. And the cool thing that Christians understand is that Jesus forgives our sins—regardless of what we've done—when we repent and commit our lives to him. He is the one who helps us live joyfully every day . . . even in eternity.

What the Bible says. ". . . Man is destined to die once, and after that to face judgment . . ." (Hebrews 9:27).

Crystals

What it's all about. Many New Agers believe that clear quartz crystals are a symbol of coming into alignment with cosmic harmony. They think that a piece of clear quartz radiates with divine white light and that by seeing, touching, wearing, using, or meditating with these crystals, one can actually work with that light in a physical form and facilitate the growth of a person's awareness.

Why crystals can't solve your problems. Think about it: spiritual awareness attained through a rock? Sounds sorta silly, doesn't it? The idea that crystals can protect or heal you is simply a lie. Whether sewn into the seam of a pair of jeans or hung in a car, a crystal is just a cool-looking rock and doesn't have any kind of power. Some teens actually carry a crystal to school, hoping it will help them do better on a test. This is foolish.

There is no biblical reason to believe in a New Age idea of psychic energy pervading the universe. Though we do believe in demonic energy that can work through occult practices, there is no reasonable basis to cause us to hold that crystals have inherent properties that make them transmitters of demonic power.

The fact is, crystals are a part of God's creation, which he pronounced good at the time he made it. There is nothing inherently occultic or spiritually dangerous about crystals, and if a Christian is interested in or attracted to them, he or she should be able to pursue this interest or attraction in good conscience.

What the Bible says. "If any of you lacks wisdom, he should ask God, who gives generously to all without finding fault, and it will be given to him" (James 1:5).

Horoscopes

What it's all about. These seemingly innocent bits of advice that appear in newspapers every day are a form of astrology, which is rooted in the New Age movement. Astrology is viewed as one of the ways to "develop your consciousness and spirituality" and "establish a means of communication with your Higher Self."

Why it's a dose of bad news. According to the Bible, astrology is in the same league as channeling . . . and both are off-limits to Christians.

Humans don't have to look to the stars for answers about life or the future. We can look to the one who made them—God. Getting people to search creation for answers rather than ask the Creator is a deception of the Devil. And according to the Word of God, horoscopes represent a doorway to a spiritual dimension that God forbids us to enter.

What the Bible says. "They are prophesying to you false visions, divinations, idolatries and the delusions of their own minds" (Jeremiah 14:14).

Occult-related games

What it's all about. On the surface, they appear to be innocent games that offer harmless fun. They come in a variety of forms: Ouija boards, crystal balls, tarot cards, and games, such as Kabala, E.S.P., Telepathy, or Dungeons and Dragons.

Why these are the Devil's toys. Each of these games has its roots in the occult. Understand that when your hands are on a Ouija board or when you cast spells during an episode of Dungeons and Dragons, you are not engaging in activities that glorify God. Play with these "toys," and you are at the mercy of the demon spirits behind them.

Instead spend time with God and seek him. Through Jesus you will find healing and the best life you've ever imagined. Remember, there is only one God and one mediator between God and man—Jesus Christ.

What the Bible says. "It is the LORD your God you must follow, and him you must revere. Keep his commands and obey him; serve him and hold fast to him" (Deuteronomy 13:4).

ON YOUR OWN

1. Read Genesis 3:1–7. What did Satan promise Adam and Eve if they ate the forbidden fruit?

2. Was this promise actually fulfilled when they did eat it?

3. Read Acts 14:8–18. What did these two solid missionaries do when the crowd acclaimed them as gods?

4. Jot down how you think Paul and Barnabas would have responded to the New Age belief that "we can become gods by transforming our consciousness."

WITH A GROUP

1. Have you ever been in a classroom situation in which something "weird" happened?

2. Share some New Age ozone experiences you've had outside the classroom (like at the mall, the doctor's office, et cetera).

3. Discuss what's most dangerous about the New Age movement.

4. Why should Christians not fear the power behind it?

5. What's the best way you can respond to the New Age (and steer others from this deadly trap)?

Media Muck

Scene one, take one:
　　"So . . . do you want the concert ticket or what?!" Lance blasts.

Ben pulls his nose out of a *Sports Illustrated* and sits up on his bed. "Well, ah, who'd ya say is performing?"

Josh—who is mechanically thunking a Nerf ball against Ben's DC Talk poster—suddenly perks up and joins the conversation. "It's only THE jam of the century . . . THE ultimate rock experience everyone at school has been talking about," he says, handing Ben his Discman and headphones. "We're talkin' the one, the only, Handguns 'N' Dead Daisies, in their historic 'Annihilate Your World' tour."

Ben slips the headphones on and cranks up the volume as he listens to the first song.

"Oh," Ben says with a grimace, punching the off button. "I know these guys. They're the ones who prance around in their underwear on stage, sacrificing live goldfish."

"It only happened once," Lance says defensively. "They're really not that rowdy."

"Not rowdy?!" Ben gasps. "Then whadda they mean by '*Rat-tat-tat-tat-tat-tat-tat/Never hesitate to put a cop on his* back/Annihilate 'em all/Annihilate your world'? And I saw one of their music videos on MTV. It was totally pornographic."

"Look, it's just music," Josh says. "You're the only guy I know who sounds like my parents. Why do you make such a big deal outta stuff that doesn't matter?"

"Yeah . . . don't be so lame," Lance adds. "It's not like this stuff is gonna turn you into a rapist or something. The band is cool, and every guy on campus listens to them. What's *your* problem?"

Lame?! MY problem?! I sound like . . . parents?! Ben panics inside (his internal geek alert running full tilt). *Where do I begin? What do I say? How do I make these guys understand just what's really wrong?*

Scene two, take one:

Jan is busy flipping through the channels on her TV, one right after the other. Susan is scrunched in a corner of the sofa, with her eyes glued to a fashion article titled "Babe Alert! Hollywood's Hunkiest."

Lisa, on the other hand, is sprawled out in a beanbag chair, pondering the mysteries of her teenage life. *Miserable. Why is my life so miserable?* she asks herself. *Why do the perfect "model-type" cover girls with the perfect figures get all the attention? Why am I NOT one of them? . . . And what's up with New Kids on the Block? Will they ever make a comeback?*

Lisa raises her head and scans the room, then rolls her eyes. *And what's wrong with this picture? We're pathetic.*

Jan suddenly begins waving the remote and exclaiming, "Ooh, ooh, ooh . . . come watch, everybody! This is my favorite talk show—'Oprah Jessy Donahue.' She has the best gossip on the tube!"

"Pathetic," Lisa mumbles as she squints at the TV. "That's all I can say . . . pathetic!"

"GREED! PASSION! MURDER!" announces the talk show host. "IT'S A STORY OF TWO JELL-O WRESTLING CIRCUS MIDGETS . . . AND A SCANDAL THAT ROCKED ORGANIZED RELIGION. . . ."

"Sick!" Lisa protests. "Change the channel, Jan. I'm not watchin' that trash."

"Oh, loosen up, Lis," Susan says. "It's fun entertainment. We know it's not real, but it's fun to watch anyway."

Earth to God, Lisa prays as she flops back on the beanbag chair. *Just what IS wrong with this picture? And how do I tell them without looking like a prude?*

ULTIMATE GEEK RESPONSES

- Give in to your friends' arguments so you'll look cool. (Even act like you enjoy the talk show.) *After all,* you reason, *it is just entertainment.*
- Recite twenty-seven Scripture passages (consecutively), then hold your friends in a headlock until they promise to change their media diet.
- Say something like, "Hey, I don't think we should hang out anymore. I don't want the stench of what you feed your mind to contaminate me."
- Shrug your shoulders and allow your pals to feed on whatever comes their way. (In other words, do nothing.)

A BETTER RESPONSE

Every day, we're bombarded with an unhealthy menu of mixed messages from TV shows, movies, books, music, even computer programs. Our brains are constantly pumped with the same lies:

- "You're nothin' unless you are having nonstop sex, possess a bank vault burstin' with bucks, have the IQ of Einstein, and are blessed with a knockout bod."
- "Look out for numero uno."
- "Go for the gusto and get all you can . . . 'cause you only live once."

The fact is, whatever fills a person on the inside will eventually become visible on the outside. As we take in media muck, we eventually live it out. So how can you geek-proof your daily mass media diet? How can you help your friends do the same?

> "Only the morally courageous are worthy of speaking to their fellow men for two hours in the dark. And only the artistically incorrupt will earn and keep the people's trust."
>
> FRANK CAPRA,
> THE NAME ABOVE THE TITLE,
> 1971

The key is to sort out the trash and focus on the treasure. Or in the words of our famous friend at *Brio* and *Breakaway*, Bob DeMoss, former youth culture specialist at Focus on the Family: "Learn to discern."

Bob says, "Distinguishing positive, edifying entertainment from that which offends God starts with a Scriptural standard. Make every effort to steer clear of destructive philosophies promoted by the media. Remember, the decisions you make today can have lifelong implications. And what goes into your brain, eventually comes out in the form of behavior."

Sure, discerning isn't a simple task, but it's not impossible. The key is to *know why* being picky with the press (and the movies and music) is important, to *know what* to be picky about, then to *take a stand* (in a way that will make your friends want to follow).

Start by following this five-point plan:

1. ***Evaluate your media diet.*** Sit down with a couple of your Christian friends and compare the lyrics of your

favorite tunes—or the messages in popular mags, movies, and TV shows—to the standards of the Bible.

Use Philippians 4:8 as a guide to evaluating the messages entering your eyes and ears: "Finally, brothers, whatever is true, whatever is noble, whatever is right, whatever is pure, whatever is lovely, whatever is admirable—if anything is excellent or praiseworthy—think about such things."

2. *Ask some hard questions.*

- *Is it TRUE?* Does this movie mock what God says is good?
- *Is it NOBLE?* Does this book help me to develop a proper mind-set?
- *Is it RIGHT?* Is this TV program causing me to compromise biblical truths?
- *Is it PURE?* Is this concert full of too much more trash than treasure to make it worth my while?
- *Is it LOVELY?* Would I be embarrassed if my youth leader found out I read this mag?
- *Is it ADMIRABLE?* Does this tune offer wisdom and (or) benefit me in any way?
- *Is it EXCELLENT?* Is this the best possible way that I could spend my time?
- *Is it PRAISEWORTHY?* Am I drawn closer to God because of this?

3. *Understand that you are what you eat.* Every song, book, and movie has a philosophy. Some are into hedonism ("Get high, have sex, and party hardy!"), others preach politics ("Kill the cops and overthrow the system!"), still others promote pessimism and despair ("Life is meaningless!"). Obviously, the argument "It's just harmless entertainment . . . it doesn't affect me" simply isn't true.

4. *Consider the source.* The primary source of mass media messages in the world—indirectly or directly—is Satan. The philosophies of the world—all the glitter and

glamour, not to mention those looking-out-for-numero-uno, shop-'til-you-drop, go-for-the-gusto attitudes—aren't from God.

5. **Find a Christian alternative.** For every bit of muck the world offers, there are quality alternatives:

- Enjoy reading hot-looking mags? Try two cool publications from Focus on the Family: *Brio* (for girls) or *Breakaway* (for guys). Or get your hands on *Campus Life* (for both).
- Love music videos? Tune in to "CCM-TV" (Family Channel), "Light Music" (Acts Network), "Real Videos" (Trinity Broadcasting Network), "Signal Exchange" (New Inspirational Network), "Solid Rock VDO" (Acts Network), or an entire network dedicated to Christian music: Z Music.
- Head to your local Christian bookstore for the best in Bibles, devotional guides, novels (not to mention TONS of nonfictional books on TONS of topics . . . like geek-proofing your faith), music resources, videos, and computer programs.

ARE CHRISTIANS NARROW-MINDED?

Here's a hard-to-swallow but true fact: when a Christian takes a stand for morality, the world hardly ever applauds. Instead many groups and individuals point an angry finger and yell stuff like, "Hate-monger!" "Bible-thumper!" "Narrow-minded, hyperconservative fundamentalist!"

Case in point. During the early nineties, musicians like Prince and Madonna stirred up controversy over their sexually explicit lyrics and recurring themes of "erotic love as religious experience." Prince's music drew heavy fire from Tipper Gore, wife of then Senator Albert Gore Jr. (Democrat, Tennessee). She and other concerned citizens sent a strong message to Washington: "Enough is enough!"

They lobbied to have warning stickers placed on albums with explicit lyrics. That's when some groups—including the media—began yelling, "Censorship! We gotta stop those conservatives!"

A search for answers. Before long some well-meaning college students, ministers, and professors got together in an attempt to "diffuse the bomb." They held a conference on "the theology of popular music" at Duke University. Their goal: use the tunes of Prince, Madonna, and Michael Jackson in order to help bridge the gap between "the temporal world of teens and the spirit-filled world of higher values."

> "In the last few years, the most influential leaders of the entertainment industry have gone beyond an admirable openness to dark and disturbing material: they have demonstrated a powerful (and puzzling) preference for the perverse."
>
> MICHAEL MEDVED,
> HOLLYWOOD VS. AMERICA,
> 1992

In other words, rather than endorsing what they thought was religious censorship, they wanted to sift through the trash and pull out the gems.

After viewing music video clips, such as Madonna's "Like a Prayer" and Prince's "Purple Rain," one minister noted, "These performers are 'preaching,' in that they are uttering an uplifting word, a healing word, to those who are their audience."

A professor had this to say: "I was initially shocked by the images in Madonna's video. But after looking at it more closely, I began to see theological principles.... I don't think antirock crusades should blind parents and ministers to the theological messages in some popular music. Let's look to the larger significance of the artists' music.... Young people really see many of these popular musicians as preachers, as messianic figures."

143

The problem. In the case of these artists, it's simply too difficult to untangle the truth from the trash. What's more, considering their track record, would you really trust a message "preached" to you by Prince or Madonna? So as you learn to discern, and as you make every effort to separate the truth from the trash, consider the stand an artist (or movie director or magazine editor) has taken in the past before you buy what they're selling today.

FREEDOM OF EXPRESSION?

The First Amendment to the United States Constitution guarantees our freedom to worship, assemble peacefully, and express our opinions both verbally and through the press. It states:

> Congress shall make no law respecting an establishment of religion, or prohibiting the free exercise thereof; or abridging the freedom of speech, or of the press; or the right of the people peaceably to assemble, and to petition the Government for a redress of grievance.

But the question is, does the First Amendment protect material deemed offensive or explicit? Where do citizens draw the line and say, "This stuff is harmful to society. We must be protected from it." Welcome to the debate of the century. (Lawmakers and social activists have been arguing this topic for eons.)

Nonetheless, some take a hard-line view and believe that freedom of expression "should not be censored in *any* way." They claim that even the stickering of music recordings with advisories, or the editing of obscenities from songs, violates First Amendment principles. What should you do?

FOUR WAYS TO DEFUSE THE "CENSORSHIP ARGUMENT"

1. *Voice YOUR rights.* Point out that the First Amendment also protects *your* right to express *your* views.

2. *Take the lid off the trash.* (The smell inside should speak for itself!) Point to a song's lyrics (or a movie's plot) and expose the bottom-line message.

3. *Ask some hard questions.* "What value is there in movies, music, and mags that glamorize violence or rape? How can we benefit from material that demoralizes any segment of society, such as songs or photo spreads that present women as sexual toys? Isn't it destructive to our society's well-being to allow a band to promote gang activity, cop killing, or suicide?"

4. *Clear the air.* Explain that taking a stand for responsible expression does not mean you support unrestrained censorship. Say something like, "As an American, I value our constitutional rights and freedoms—and I DON'T support censorship. The key word is 'responsibility.' Ensuring true freedom means ensuring the safety, well-being, and future for *every* person, not allowing irresponsible behavior that could ultimately destroy our freedom."

PLAY BY PLAY—WHAT'S RIGHT, WHAT'S WRONG

Channel surfing

The right frequency. Ninety-eight percent of American households have at least one TV set. Television zaps you with instant information. It also educates and entertains in a powerful way.

Warning signals. But be careful. TV is often a box of bad values and is more dangerous than you think. It is subtle and worldly, and it's hard to convince TV watchers that they are glued to something that, in the long run, may do them great spiritual damage.

- The American Academy of Pediatrics reports that the average child will view more than twenty thousand commercials during the thirteen hundred hours of TV programming he or she consumes annually.

- TV standards have reached an all-time low. What was forbidden in the golden age of the tube (bedroom scenes, "light" cussing) is now commonplace.
- Anti-Christian hostility is often reflected on the tube in two ways: (1) censorship of a positive portrayal of Christians in a modern-day setting; (2) presentation of modern-day Christians, nearly without exception, in a negative manner.

Hollywood's blockbuster bombs

The right frequency. Okay, I (Mike) can't deny it. I love movies. Give me a tub of popcorn, a Coke, and a date with the latest video thriller or big-screen drama, and I'm a happy man.

The cool side of celluloid is that:

- like a good novel, it can offer good, clean entertainment
- movies can sweep you away to far-off adventures, tug at your emotions, and stir your heart to action
- like TV, movies educate in a powerful way

Warning signals. As you're well aware, there is a definite uncool side to the celluloid biz. And there have been many times—waaay too many times—when I kick back to a blockbuster feast . . . and get furious (not to mention heartburn).

Like moments when:

- my ears are blasted with foul, four-letter words
- my eyes fog up from lusty sex scenes
- the screen drips with gallons of blood and gore

- human life is blown away as casually as you'd buy a pack of gum
- the things God says are valuable—like love, purity, holiness, and integrity—are mocked and made fun of

More and more movie critics are giving Hollywood a "thumbs-down." Check out what Michael Medved—the host of "Sneak Previews," a popular program on PBS—has to say about the industry:

> As a working film critic, I've watched this assault on traditional values for more than a decade. Not only have I endured six or seven movies every week, year after year, but I've also received a steady stream of letters from moviegoers who are upset. . . . The most significant shapers of the entertainment industry, in their quest for artistic legitimacy, have adopted a view of the world that is surprisingly dark, even desperate, highlighting elements of chaos, cruelty, and random violence.

Wacked-out discman

The right frequency. Most teens would agree: life without music would be pretty boring. Stop by your local sound source and you're bombarded with choices: live concert recordings, limited-edition tour fan packs, rereleases of rereleased classics (recorded on recycled tape).

If you love music videos but think MTV and VH–1 are your only cable choices, start "channel surfing" . . . and check out what's jammin' on Christian networks. It's definitely the age of music videos, and nearly every Christian musician has gotten in on the act. The stars on these videos not only give you all the cool sounds and cutting-edge images that other networks offer but something else as well: positive messages. The world of music TV—Christian-style—is beamed into your home via one of a half dozen or

> "Not all rap is bad; in fact, much of it is brilliant. But more and more, the good stuff is being overshadowed by a torrent of obscene lyrics and graphic videos.... 'Gangsta rap' often denigrates women and glorifies guns and gangs."
>
> NATHAN MCCALL,
> "MY RAP AGAINST RAP,"
> WASHINGTON POST,
> NOVEMBER 13, 1993

so cable programs, even via a whole network.

Warning signals. Watch out for the wacked-out messages from certain secular artists.

Suicide and murder plays big in some gansta rap and heavy-metal tunes. Not long ago a clique of Missouri adolescents murdered their friend, then pleaded insanity brought on by their involvement with satanism via heavy-metal music.

The violent messages of rap persuaded a D.C. youth to enter the world of gangs. Check out his story: "The message I picked up was: if somebody double-crosses you, he deserves to die.... At age nineteen, I gunned down a man. It was like one great fantasy, as glorious as the gangland slayings in the movies and rap tunes.... It may seem crazy to tie music to behavior ... but street rap is more than rhyming words. The key element is aggression—in the rappers' body language, tone, and witty rhymes—that often leaves listeners hyped, on edge, angry."

ON YOUR OWN

1. Check out 2 Corinthians 6:4–7:1. List the key qualities, attitudes, and behaviors Jesus expects of Christians. Why is it dangerous to be "yoked" with those who don't share our values? How do you think this applies to media muck?

2. Now flip over to Galatians 5:19–21 and read.

From this passage, list the acts of the sinful nature:

Jot down the warning (see verse 21):

3. Now read Galatians 5:22–25.
   From this passage, list the fruit of the Spirit:

Jot down the challenge (see verse 25):

4. How has the media shaped your attitudes? List below the ways that a certain song or movie fueled wrong behavior or a bad habit. (Be honest!)

5. List three ways that we can keep in step with the Holy Spirit.

WITH A GROUP

1. Pick an athlete in any sport and list the types of food that would give him or her energy . . . and the kinds that would slow him or her down.

2. "Garbage in, garbage out" is a true observation. Why is it—and how is it—that what goes in, eventually comes out?

3. Why, do you think, does entertainment have such a powerful hold on our society?

4. How has a tune or a movie influenced you in the past?

5. Name some things that your group can do to combat TV programs and movies that ridicule Christian beliefs and seek to undermine your faith.

12

Unreality Lives!

We know you're ready to get the book over with. But there's one more VERY IMPORTANT thing to talk about.

Though the issues we're going to cover may not apply to *everyone* reading these pages, one thing we've learned from our years of being teenagers—and our years of working with them—is this: unreality loves to take up residence in the mind of a teen—even a Christian teen.

What kind of unreality are we talking about? Well, it's different for girls and guys. It seems each gender has a tendency to glue themselves onto their own unique type of fantasy. And guys and gals sometimes get *stuck* in unreality.

Before we talk about what it tends to be for each sex, a word about fantasy

First, there's the harmless variety.

For example, dreaming of being an airplane pilot, a pro athlete, President of the United States, an Olympic champion, a war hero, a doctor or nurse, a missionary or pastor—these are all safe fantasies. Safe because, to a degree, they are all possible. That is, most are goals worth dreaming about. Fantasizing about what it would be like to one day dunk over Shaquille O'Neal may not get you to the NBA, but by motivating you to pursue and work toward that athletic dream, it may lead to a college scholarship, or plant within you a hunger to teach or coach.

What starts as a childhood dream often leads to a very fulfilling career.

Then there's the not-so-harmless variety . . .

Christian geeks are made, not born. The Enemy has a long track record of success in slowly polluting the mind of the young Christian. It's not childish, childhood fantasies he wants young believers to dream about, it's adult-type, potentially lifetime addiction to unreality he wants Christians to swallow.

He starts by planting seeds early in a person's life. He waters these seeds through repetitive temptations until they begin to sprout. Then he sits back and watches as one of them grows so large it consumes the once pure and naive follower of Christ.

He attacks us in our weakest areas, and these areas are different for girls and guys.

FOR GIRLS IT'S THE HUNGER FOR ROMANCE

Disney, of course, has known this for decades. *Sleeping Beauty, Cinderella, The Little Mermaid*, and other movies present girls as able to be happy and fulfilled only if they have a man to call their own. And once they have one, their life is complete.

Since TV began, afternoon and nighttime soap operas have daily kept the romantic fires burning for teenage girls, housewives, and working women (those who own VCRs).

For some, knowing the love life of their favorite characters borders on obsession.

Also on the list of romance inducers are the hundreds of "romance novels" that girls read. I (Greg) once knew a Christian girl who would read two or three per week. At age nineteen she thought she had met her handsome hero. A man in the service swept her off her feet, and they were married in less than two months.

Were her romantic dreams fulfilled? Not even close. The first week of marriage was a nightmare as they traveled to his next post of duty. For three months, they lived in a mobile home while he went to work every day. When she realized that her man wasn't the one she had been fantasizing about, she sought—and got—an annulment. The marriage was over.

Two years later she thought she had found her REAL lifetime lover. He was a strong Christian, too. Within a year she had divorced him. Not able to handle the guilt, she completely ditched her once-strong faith in pursuit of the ideal guy. The bar scene is where she ended up, going from one guy to the next.

Extreme story, you think? Perhaps. But maybe not. The more likely scenario that Satan orchestrates happens something like this: Thoughts that a man is the answer to a girl's life are fueled through the sources just mentioned. She finds a man who loves her and treats her right. They get engaged, get married, start a home, begin to have kids ... everything is perfect and ideal, right? Just like the movies. Except that what happens is that the man gets busy with work, she gets busy with work or the kids; and pretty soon, familiarity breeds contempt. The handsome prince turns out to be a normal guy ... and the pressures of daily survival make her wonder if she's missed something along the way.

Perhaps there's a better life out there somewhere, she thinks.

Millions of women—Christian women—have these thoughts. (Go ahead, ask a few.) But instead of leaving their family and running away with someone else, most (but not all) simply stay married and try to survive their unfulfilled expectations about men and romance.

Romance is great. Marriage IS wonderful. Some men do turn out to be quality guys. But when a girl places unreal expectations on a member of the male species—ideas that he has the ability to endlessly fulfill the romantic fantasies of his mate—her dreams WILL be shattered. Only ONE man ever promised to bring "life in all its fullness" to us humans (male or female): Jesus Christ. Nowhere in the Bible is it promised that a man will make a woman's life complete. The reason is because it's an unreal expectation. It CAN'T happen.

Ah, but that's not what soap operas, movies, and novels say, right?

FOR GUYS IT'S AN ILLICIT ATTRACTION TO THE OPPOSITE SEX

Illicit means improper, prohibited, unlawful, or unauthorized.

You may not have been aware that there's an alarm clock built into every guy. At the right point in our maturity, it goes off. We open our eyes . . . shake our heads and say, "Girls are different! Good job, God!"

For each guy, that alarm clock goes off at a different time (usually between the ages of eleven and fifteen). Those feelings are nothing we can conjure up or manufacture. God gave them to us; they're normal, right, and really one of God's best ideas.

Waking up to females is what we call an *innocent* attraction. It's a wonderful realization. But what happens with guys about this same time isn't so wonderful. Satan tries everything he can to take the wonder and innocence out and put obsession and illicitness in. What fuels a male's obsession? It's different for each guy, but here are a few places where it begins:

- Friends at school start talking about body parts. (We've already covered this one, so we won't talk about it again.)
- TV shows or commercials not only talk about it, they reveal a lot more skin than you'd *ever* see . . . unless you lived at the beach.
- Ditto for movies—even the covers of videos from the corner video store are provocative.
- Billboards.
- Swimsuit issues in male sports magazines.

So far, you might be thinking, I can't escape this stuff, so what are you getting to?

- Pornography.

This is the place Satan wants it all to lead to, guys. His strategy is to take the normal, innocent attraction of what's reality for guys and turn it into an illicit obsession in unrealityland. He's patient but unrelenting. Viewing pictures or videos of naked women keeps *Christian* men—by the thousands—frustrated, guilt-ridden, and unable to live in reality as it relates to the true desires of the female in their life.

Plus it's addictive. That's right. Like any drug, pornography is progressive; the more you look, the more you want. And soon you'll want different, increasingly disgusting or violent forms.

It's beyond the scope of this book to detail to someone who is already hooked by this stuff how to get off it. Our goal is to warn you that this seed Satan sows into the mind of a man is the most destructive and fastest-growing seed the Enemy plants. Once in bloom, it fuels unreal thoughts about sex, thoughts that can severely hinder the lifetime of enjoyment God wants you to have with one woman for the rest of your life.

Yes, that's a pretty heavy statement, but it's true. If you don't believe us, show these words to a trusted adult and ask him how many men he knows—older men in their thirties and forties—who are still in bondage to this stuff. We're not blowing smoke on this one, guys. There are Christian male sex addicts in our churches, and their sickness didn't just happen to start in their post-teenage years. For most, it started "innocently" or "accidentally." They found pornographic material on the side of the road, a neighbor or an older brother had it, perhaps some guy brought it to school. Pornography is everywhere.

If you haven't allowed your eyes to feast on this stuff as of yet—or if you've just looked a few times—we challenge you to make perhaps the toughest commitment of your life: commit to NEVER willingly gaze at this stuff, for as long as you live. If there's a "life mission" that a man must have, it's to keep his mind pure from images that will rob him of the wonder of experiencing sex the way God intended: with a lifetime wife. This challenge is for boys who really want to become Christian men.

BACK TO REALITY

Enjoying life to its fullest means living in reality, not fantasy. Christian geekhood occurs when the teenage believer fails to recognize the seeds Satan is trying to sow during these adolescent years.

This is one area where the Christian teen likely WON'T look like a geek during his or her teenage years. The consequences of living in unreality won't occur until later in life. But the potential for long-term unhappiness is incredible. Many adults' downward spiral didn't begin in their twenties, it began during their teens.

Please! Don't let that downward spiral begin during yours. Live in reality today, and you'll enjoy the reality God wants to give you the rest of your life.

ON YOUR OWN

1. Rank the other areas where people at your school try to live in unreality:

   _____ Gambling

   _____ Pursuing unrealistic goals

   _____ Drinking

   _____ Fantasy role-playing games

   _____ Drugs

   _____ Other:

2. What do these passages say about the real kingdom Jesus is from?

   ✎ John 18:36

   ✎ John 6:15

   ✎ Matthew 26:53

3. Living in unreality means being in the dark when it comes to living in reality. What do these passages say about what God wants to do with those who live in darkness?

   ✎ Luke 1:77–79

   ✎ 1 Peter 2:9

   ✎ John 12:46

4. What are people naturally attracted to?

   ✎ John 3:19

   ✎ John 7:7

5. What happens when we walk in darkness?

   ✎ John 12:35–36

WITH A GROUP

1. Answer the questions above.
2. Why, do you think, do people walk into the world of unreality?
3. What can you do for a pre-Christian you know who is living in an unreal or fantasy world?
4. What can you do when you see a Christian living in unreality?
5. What is the best way you can identify reality so you don't drift into the world of unreality?

RESOLVING "CONTRADICTIONS" IN THE BIBLE

The next time someone asks you about a contradiction in the Bible, you can be prepared to give an answer.

by Ronald Youngblood

Several years ago when I was an interim pastor, a member of my congregation came to my office greatly agitated. He'd learned that a seminary instructor had said some numbers in the Old Testament are simply estimates, and he was concerned that this cast doubt on the Bible's inerrancy.

The verse in question had to do with a battle in Judges 20:46, which the casualty count is given as 25,000.

I asked, "Don't you think 25,000 could have been a round number—that the count was somewhere between 23,000 and 27,000?"

My friend insisted this couldn't be so.

"Well, what would be reasonable from your standpoint?" I asked. "That it was somewhere between 24,000 and 26,000?"

"No."

"Somewhere between 24,990 and 25,010?"

"No."

"How about between 24,999 and 25,001?" I asked. "Or are you saying it has to be right on the money?"

"Well . . . yes."

In those days, the war in Vietnam was in the news daily. "The casualty counts in the newspapers are obviously estimates. Why can't it be that way in the Bible?" I asked.

"Because the daily paper isn't my Bible," he replied.

"Good enough. But what if I showed you two verses in the Old Testament, both describing the same incident, where different figures are used?" I asked.

"Is that right? Are there such passages?"

At this point, I showed him the story of King David's census of fighting men, which is recorded twice: in 2 Samuel 24 and in 1 Chronicles 21. In the first account, Joab reports to the king: "In Israel there were eight hundred thousand able-bodied men who could handle a sword, and in Judah five hundred thousand" (verse 9).

This 1.3 million total in Samuel does not square precisely with the same story in Chronicles. There Joab reports a different number of men to David: "In all Israel there were one million one hundred thousand men who could handle a sword, including four hundred and seventy thousand in Judah" (verse 5).

When we closed the Bible, my friend sighed with relief. "I'm glad we've talked," he said. "It takes a big weight off my shoulders. I'd always wondered why counts in the Bible come out in round numbers so often."

I think of my friend when I encounter other Christians who are disturbed by similar apparent discrepancies in Scripture. Sometimes, simple explanations can relieve the concern over verses that are puzzling or seem to contradict each other.

THE FEEDING OF FIVE THOUSAND AND THE FEEDING OF FOUR THOUSAND

Some people are troubled by what they see as contradictions in the numbers of people who were fed loaves and fish at one event. The explanation is simple: Mark is describing separate occasions.

By reading carefully through the two passages (Mark 6:30–44; 8:1–10), we can see how the details of the incidents differ. In the earlier account, Jesus was met by a crowd on the shore after he had been with his disciples in a boat. In the later incident, the crowd had been with Jesus for three days.

Moreover, different numbers of loaves and fishes were divided on the two occasions. Jesus discusses these as two separate incidents in Mark 8:18–20:

> "And don't you remember? When I broke the five loaves for the five thousand, how many basketfuls of pieces did you pick up?"
> "Twelve," they replied.
> "And when I broke the seven loaves for the four thousand, how many basketfuls of pieces did you pick up?"
> They answered, "Seven."

TWO PROVERBS THAT APPEAR TO GIVE CONTRADICTORY ADVICE

Proverbs 26:4 says, "Do not answer a fool according to his folly, or you will be like him yourself," but the very next verse says, "Answer a fool according to his folly, or he will be wise in his own eyes."

Are we to answer the fool or not?

Each situation requires a judgment call, the inspired writer is really saying. On one hand, if you answer a fool according to his folly, you may be stooping to his level. On the other hand, if you don't, he may think he is wise, and you will have missed an opportunity to denounce his foolishness.

There is no perfect solution when dealing with a fool. Here are two suggestions (not ironclad rules). A believer must discern which is applicable in different situations.

It's important to understand the source of proverbs and how they should be read. The wise men or sages associated with the Wisdom Books were an important force in Israelite society (Jeremiah 18:18). They were called on to give advice to kings and also to instruct the young.

While prophets tended to deal with the religious side of life, the wise men were concerned about everyday matters. Therefore we must not interpret the book of Proverbs as prophecy, or its statements about certain cause-and-effect relationships as promises.

The situation is somewhat akin to maxims your grandmother might have given you. "A stitch in time saves nine," she'd sometimes say, admonishing you not to delay. But at other times, she'd warn, "Haste makes waste." This conflicting advice didn't cause a problem, because you understood Granny's common sense. Either motto might be appropriate in a given circumstance.

THE NUMBER OF WOMEN WHO WENT TO THE TOMB OF THE RESURRECTED JESUS

Because each gospel gives a detailed description of the events surrounding Jesus' crucifixion, burial, and resurrection, they present some of the most fascinating instances of alleged discrepancies in Scripture. To take a single example: did one woman (John 20:1), two (Matthew 28:1), three (Mark 16:1), or five or more (Luke 24:10) go to the empty tomb on that first Easter Sunday morning?

First, we observe that none of the gospel writers insists that the woman (women) he mentions was (were) the only one (ones) present. In fact, John implies that Mary Magdalene was not alone, because he quotes her as saying, concerning Jesus, "We don't know where they have put him!" (John 20:2).

It's entirely possible that the women came to the tomb at various times and from various places in the city so they would not arouse suspicion or attract attention. We should not assume that they all came at once or from the same place.

Perhaps Mary Magdalene went to the tomb first (as recorded by John). She was soon joined by Mary the mother of James (as Matthew implies), then by Salome (Mark's account), and finally by Joanna and one or more other women (Luke's gospel). Such a reconstruction accounts for the differences without needlessly turning them into contradictions.

ACCOUNTS IN JOSHUA, OF ISRAEL'S CONQUEST OF CANAAN, THAT SEEM TO BE CONTRADICTED IN JUDGES

Joshua tells of the blitzkrieg conquest of Canaan. It presents an optimistic picture of what took place during six years (at most) as it relates the series of victories—in central, southern, and northern Canaan—that gave the Israelites control of all the hill country and the Negev.

Then we open the book of Judges, which indicates things were not as rosy as they first seemed. Chapters 1 and 2 describe mopping-up operations, then give us a list of towns that were not taken because the conquerors were sinful.

Why these differing accounts? It has to do with the way things appeared at the times the books were written.

The discussion in Joshua of the conquest of the land was accurate—as far as it went. It was only later, at the time of Judges, that pockets of resistance were found. The earlier conquest was as complete as it needed to be (Joshua), but some towns had to be recaptured later on (Judges).

TWO ACCOUNTS OF JUDAS' SUICIDE

According to Matthew 27:5, Judas "went away and hanged himself," but in Acts 1:18 we read that he "fell headlong, his body burst open and all his intestines spilled out."

This is an example of an apparent contradiction we can resolve with an understanding of biblical culture and the ways that words are translated.

In our culture, "hanging from a tree" suggests a scene from a TV western in which a lynch mob puts a noose around someone's neck. The victim is killed by strangulation, "hanging from a tree."

But this was not a form of execution in biblical times; the common method was impaling on a post. Following impalement, the body would be displayed as a warning to others.

To understand the story of Judas' suicide, we must know what its key words signified. The word *hanged* meant "impaled," and *tree* was a wooden pole on which the body was hung after execution.

Even the New Testament reference to Christ's crucifixion "Cursed is everyone who is hung on a tree" (Galatians 3:13) was talking about hanging as a form of impaling (spikes were driven into Christ's body). And the "tree" was the wooden pole, or cross.

So the two accounts of Judas' death are not at odds. It seems his "hanging" was an impalement caused when he jumped (or fell) onto a sharpened post.

Apparent contradictions in the Bible, such as these, are few and far between, but they deserve our attention.

For thousands of years, Scripture has proved itself to be totally trustworthy and absolutely authoritative. The burden of proof, then, is on the person claiming to find a contradiction, who must demonstrate that it has no reasonable explanation.

And for believers, discovering possible explanations for these "contradictions" can lead to greater understanding, appreciation, and conviction concerning the Bible.*

*This article first appeared in the September 1986 issue of *Moody* magazine. Used by permission.

WHAT ARE YOUR RIGHTS ON CAMPUS?

Here are some resources to help you start or lead a Christian club on campus:

The Christian Club Guide ($2.95) by Randy Brantley and Dave Hughey.

> The Christian Club Campaign
> P.O. Box 552
> Little Rock, AR 72203
> (501) 376–4791, ext. 5132

Club Handbook ($25.00) by Ray Hollis, Student Evangelism Handbook.

> Youth America Campus Clubs
> P.O. Box 20,000
> Oklahoma City, OK 73156
> (405) 947–2000

Take a Stand: Campus Ministry Manual for Students ($5.00) and *12-Minute Meetings for Campus Christian Clubs* (call for price) by Jeff Swaim.

> Youth Alive Campus
>   Ministry
> 1445 Booneville
>   Avenue
> Springfield, MO 65802
> (800) 545–2766

If you're looking for legal materials, try these:

The Equal Access Act and the Public Schools: Q & A (booklet; first copy free).

Christian Legal Society
4208 Evergreen Lane, Suite 222
Annandale, VA 22003
(703) 642–1070

Student's Legal Rights on a Public School Campus ($10.00) by J. W. Brinkley.

Student Discipleship Ministries
P.O. Box 60134
Fort Worth, TX 76115
(817) HIS-PLAN

Students' Rights and the Public Schools and *Equal Access, Equal Rights* (free pamphlets).

American Center for Law and Justice
P.O. Box 64429
Virginia Beach, VA 23467
(804) 523–7570

Your Rights in the Public Schools ($5.00) by John W. Whitehead.

The Rutherford Institute
P.O. Box 7482
Charlottesville, VA 22906–7482
(800) 225–1791

SUGGESTED READING

Chapter 1—*Evolution*

The Illustrated Origins Answer Book, 3rd ed. by Paul S. Taylor, Eden Productions, 1991.

Chapter 2—*Friendships*

The Campus Life Guide to Making and Keeping Friends by Chris Lutes, Zondervan, 1991.

Do You Sometimes Feel Like a Nobody? by Tim Stafford, Zondervan, 1991.

Keeping Your Cool While Sharing Your Faith by Greg Johnson and Susie Shellenberger, Tyndale, 1993.

Under Siege by Josh McDowell and Chuck Klein, SonLife, 1992.

Chapter 3—*Bible Apologetics*

Don't Check Your Brains at the Door by Josh McDowell and Bob Hostetler, Word, 1992.

Know What You Believe by Paul E. Little, Victor, 1970.

Know Why You Believe by Paul E. Little, Victor, 1967.

Why Believe the Bible by John F. MacArthur Jr., Regal, 1980.

Chapter 4—*Thriving in Public School*

Friend of the Lonely Heart by Josh McDowell and Norm Wakefield, Word, 1991.

Peer Pressure: Making It Work for You by Chris Lutes, Zondervan, 1990.

Personal Best: A Campus Life Guide to Knowing and Liking Yourself by Diane Eble, Zondervan, 1991.

Welcome to High School by Diane Eble, Chris Lutes, and Kris Bearss, Zondervan, 1991.

Chapter 5—*Abortion*

Pro-Life Answers to Pro-Choice Arguments by Randy Alcorn, Multnomah, 1992.

Chapter 6—*Jobs*

We couldn't find anything, so what we wrote is obviously cutting-edge stuff.

Chapter 7—*Sexuality*

Caution: Sexual Choices May Be Hazardous to Your Health by Mary Ann Mayo, Zondervan, 1989.

Love, Sex, & the Whole Person by Tim Stafford, Zondervan, 1991.

Sex: Desiring the Best by Barry St. Clair and Bill Jones, Here's Life, 1988.

What Hollywood Won't Tell You About Love, Sex, & Dating by Greg Johnson and Susie Shellenberger, Regal, 1994.

Chapter 8—*Dating and Respect*

Dating: Picking and Being a Winner by Barry St. Clair and Bill Jones, Here's Life, 1988.

Getting Ready for the Guy/Girl Thing by Greg Johnson and Susie Shellenberger, Regal, 1992.

Love: Making It Last by Barry St. Clair and Bill Jones, Here's Life, 1988.

A Love Story by Tim Stafford, Zondervan, 1993.

13 Things You Gotta Know to Keep Your Love Life Alive & Well by Josh McDowell and Bob Hostetler, Word, 1994.

258 Great Dates While You Wait by Susie Shellenberger and Greg Johnson, Broadman & Holman, 1995.

Chapter 9—*Homosexuality*

Setting the Record Straight, Focus on the Family, 1995.

Chapter 10—*New Age*

The Many Faces of Deception by Florence Bulle, Bethany House, 1989.

Turmoil in the Toy Box by Phil Phillips, Starburst, 1986.

Understanding the New Age by Russell Chandler, Zondervan, 1993.

Chapter 11—*Media Muck*

Children at Risk by Dr. James Dobson and Gary Bauer, Word, 1990.

Hollywood vs. America by Michael Medved, HarperCollins, 1992.

Raising the Standard by Carman, Sparrow Press, 1994.

Chapter 12—*Pornography*

Again, not much out there geared toward teens.